Dotcometrics: Measuring online success

Version 1.0

Get more information at:

www.dotcometrics.com

Introduction

How do you know how well or how poorly your online business is doing? There are obvious indicators such as positive cash flows or increasing traffic trends, but exactly how well is it doing? Online ventures are unique in their difficulty in evaluating them objectively since there are usually no directly comparable competitors that can be used as a benchmark for evaluating your online success. That is where this book comes in.

Throughout this book, we take a look at various equations and their meanings in order to help the non-mathematician make sense of what is being calculated and how to use that information to make business decisions. We explain the equation, the variables that go into formulating the equation, where to get them, and what to do with the end result to enhance your business processes. By quantitatively measuring your business, you will develop an objective framework on which to base your progress that will be removed from the emotional highs and lows we all experience in running an online business.

Category: Website Visitor Behavior

1. Desired Action Percentage (DAP)

Equation: DAP = V_{DA}/V_T X 100

Where V_{DA} = number of Visitors who execute the Desired Action, and

$$V_T = \text{Total number of Visitors to the site}$$

Description: The DAP indicates the percentage of total visitors who carry out a desired action. A higher DAP indicates the action has value to visitors or you presented a more effective call to action. In effect, the DAP measures how well what you *say* you offer matches what you, in fact, *do* offer.

Example: The goal of your website (or of an individual web page) is for visitors to sign up for a free e-book. 10,000 people visited your site this month. 250 signed up for the e-book.

250/10,000 = .025, or 2.5%. Your DAP for the month is 2.5%.

Is 2.5% a good result? The answer depends on several factors. (We'll assume the desired action is the free e-book signup.) One factor is how well marketing or search engine optimization efforts result in targeted visitors. If most of your traffic comes from visitors who are already interested in your product or service, a low DAP indicates the e-book is of very little interest to the average visitor – or you did a poor job explaining its content and value. On the other hand, if the average visitor stumbles onto your site through a wide variety of sources, a low DAP may simply be indicative of the fact that you are intentionally casting a wide marketing net.

Plus, if a page has a number of different desired actions, it can be difficult to determine which visitors came for which reason. If you offer a free e-book, a free newsletter sign-up, and a paid subscription plan all on the same page, and you used a variety of marketing efforts to draw visitors, it can be tough to distinguish which "type" of visitor took which action.

A great way to use the Desired Action Percentage is to evaluate results over time. Say you want visitors to sign up for your free e-book: test a number of variables individually and compare the results. Change the placement of the sign-up box, change the wording of your PPC ads, try different SEO initiatives and each time, compare your results. A higher DAP means the change was effective; a lower DAP means it was not.

Just make sure you don't ask the DAP to do something it can't do. Say you want visitors to sign up for a free e-book, but later you hope they will sign up for a monthly subscription to your service. The percentage of visitors who sign up for the e-book has nothing to do with the percentage of visitors who sign up for a paid subscription.

Instead, you need to calculate a separate DAP for visitors who arrive at your subscription sign-up page.

Reference link: http://www.jimnovo.com/metrics-definitions.htm

2. Repeat Visitor Index (RVI)

Equation: $RVI = V_R / V_T \times 100$

Where V_R = number of Visitors who Returned to the website, and

V_T = Total number of Visitors to the website.

Description: The Repeat Visitor Index measures the percentage of visitors who return to the website after an initial visit during a specific time period.

Example: 1,000 people visited your site this month. Out of those visitors, 100 returned and visited your site again.

$100/1,000 = .1$, or 10%. Your RVI for the month is 10%.

RVI is a great way to determine whether you are successfully engaging visitors. Say you run a blog; you work hard to bring new visitors to your site. (You even spend a little money on banner ads to draw visitors.) New visitors are fine, but repeat visitors are great. Once you secure a new reader, or repeat visitor, you don't need to spend time and money attracting that reader because your content is sufficient. In short, the higher the RVI the better your website engages your average new visitor.

Think of it this way: If you run an information-based website you depend, whether you realize it or not, on repeat visitors. (Even if your ultimate goal is to sell a product or service, you're much more likely to sell to visitors who come back time after time; after all, the advertising cliché, "A person has to see an ad seven times before they'll buy," is based on real data.) You can get more total visitors by advertising more, but what if you raise your RVI? Your marketing is more efficient because you get more bang for your advertising buck. Or you could decide to lower your advertising expenditure because you are able to "convert" a higher percentage of visitors, even if the total number of visitors is reduced.

You can improve your RVI by specifically targeting your marketing, providing great content, ensuring site navigation is streamlined and intuitive, and constantly creating new content to keep the site fresh and relevant. Evaluate your results over time to measure your improvement, and the effectiveness of your marketing and content efforts.

Reference link: http://seoroi.com/case-studies/repeat-visitors-tracking-percentage-vs-absolute-numbers/

3. Average Session Length (ASL)

Equation: ASL = S_T/V_T

Where S_T = Sum of individual session Times, and

V_T = Total number of Visitors to the website.

Description: Average Session Length measures the average amount of time a visitor spends on a website or a page.

Example: 5,000 visitors came to your site this month. They spent a total of 12 hours, or 720 minutes, or 43,200 seconds on your site.

43,200/5,000 = 8.64 seconds per visitor, per session.

Sounds like the average visitor doesn't stay long, does it? Don't feel bad; in some industries the average visitor stays less than half that long. On the other hand, major online shopping sites like QVC.com and Apple.com average over nine minutes per session. It all depends on the nature of your site and your industry.

You can also use ASL to evaluate the success of changes you make to a particular process. Say you redesign your shopping cart and checkout process; if sales remain steady (or even increase) while ASL decreases, that should indicate transactions are taking place more quickly (which is a good thing for all concerned).

Keep in mind a long ASL could indicate your visitors like your content and want to stay … or it could mean they're struggling to understand your navigation scheme or are struggling to find meaningful content. In general, though, a longer ASL means you're successfully engaging your visitors.

You can use average session length to measure the effectiveness of your website, but you can also use ASL to help you determine where to place advertising. Say you want to place a banner ad; the longer a visitor stays on a page, the greater the odds they'll respond to your ad and click through, assuming, of course, that the site attracts visitors interested in your product or service in the first place. But if you sell soccer products and are choosing between different soccer-themed sites on which to place your ad, ASL could be one of the factors you initially consider. Once you've placed the ad, of course, you'll evaluate how much traffic you received and how many sales you've made – that's the true test of advertising effectiveness.

Reference link:
http://www.webmasterworld.com/webmaster/3496869.htm

4. Page Loading Time (PLT)

Equation: PLT = elapsed Time to fully Load a web Page

Description: Page Loading Time measures the total elapsed time from when a link is clicked (or a bookmark is accessed) until a page fully loads, including images and other page elements.

Example: You click a banner ad and it takes four seconds for the page to load. The PLT is four seconds.

Web visitors are notoriously fickle; make them wait and they'll leave, regardless of your content. Flash, large animated GIFs, some Java applications, and other site features can dramatically increase load times. Advertisers are also concerned with PLT because they want visitors to see their ads, not bounce away because of slow load times.

Why do fast PLTs matter?

- **Fast PLTs create a better user experience.** (Fast PLTs allow you to concentrate on content; slow PLTs make you painfully aware the page is loading slowly.)

- **PLT could affect SEO.** Google considers load times as a factor for indexing AdWords pages, and some industry insiders suspect page load times could also affect natural search engine rankings.

- **Slow pages could cost money.** Forrester Research and Gartner Group reported that, "Ecommerce sites lose $1.1 to $1.3 billion in revenue each year due to customer click-away caused by slow loading websites."

As a result, your goal is to make PLT as short as possible while still providing interesting and dynamic content. If you're considering building a new site, specify loading time parameters for your web designers to meet.

A number of free tools can be used to determine PLT. For a simple tool, try http://www.numion.com/Stopwatch/index.html. Enter a URL to find out how long it takes the page to load. For a more comprehensive tool, http://www.websiteoptimization.com/services/analyze/ provides a comprehensive breakdown of different modem and broadband speeds.

Where PLT is concerned, speed kills; if the speed is slow, that is.

Reference link:
http://www.speedyadverts.com/SATopics/html/web_site1 5.html

5. Home Page Reject Ratio (HPRR)

Equation: HPRR = V_H/ V_T X 100

Where V_H = total Visitors who leave the Home page within 30 seconds, and

V_T = Total number of Visitors to the site.

Description: The Home Page Reject Ratio measures the quality of visits. A high HPRR means visitor "value" is low.

Example: Your site registered 20,000 visitors this month. 4,000 stayed less than thirty seconds.

4,000/20,000 = .2, or 20%. Your HPRR is 20%.

Automated, non-human visitors like spiders, bots, and link checkers are not quality visitors; they simply inflate the total number of visitors to the site. Visitors who "wander by" and don't stay are also not quality visitors; they also inflate your gross numbers. Both types are non-valued visitors, at least from your point of view (although you do want the search engine spiders to come by frequently).

Why use thirty seconds as a threshold? In some ways it's an arbitrary figure; 25 seconds or 35 seconds may be just as useful. Some research indicates users who land on pages with adequate relevant content will typically need more than thirty seconds to absorb that content.

Keep in mind HPRR is directionally-accurate, but it's not an absolute measurement of the success of your home page. Weighing other factors in conjunction with HPRR is also useful. For example, you may have a high HPRR because repeat visitors quickly click on to other pages; your HPRR could be high because you run a news-oriented site and repeat visitors can determine within seconds whether new content has been added; or your ecommerce site landing page could have a high HPRR because visitors quickly move on to a specific product category on your site.

So let's keep it simple. You run what is, in effect, a one-page website; visitors who come to your home page check out your content and decide whether or not to buy one product. If your HPRR is high, your marketing may be drawing the wrong visitors or your sales page may be ineffective. Experiment with different marketing techniques and different product descriptions, and evaluate your success using HPRR.

Reference link:
http://www.publicinsite.com/Reports/churn-churn-part3.asp

6. Visitor Engagement Degree (VED)

Equation: VED = N/V

Where N = Number of page views, and

V = number of unique Visitors,

Description: In a simple form, visitor engagement can be calculated by dividing the number of page views by the total number of unique visitors to determine how "engaged" they became in the site. (We'll look more closely at the phrase "simple form" in a moment.)

Example: You receive 4,000 unique visitors this month. Total page views equal 25,000.

25,000/4,000 = 6.25 pages per visitor. Your VED is 6.25.

Now let's talk about "simple form." VED can be measured in a wide variety of ways; some equations include eight to ten variables. (Math can be fun, but that sounds like a little too much fun.) More complex calculations include factors like click depth, duration indices, loyalty indices, interaction indices, and … okay, I'll stop. Unless you're a mathematician – and even if you are – that's probably too complicated.

So, VED is one way to measure how engaged your visitors become with your site. An engaged visitor will tend to view a relatively large number of pages. Another visitor who stopped by, clicked a link or two, and then left, in all likelihood, didn't find much on your site worth pursuing. Visitors who clicked eight to ten links not only found your site useful but also will probably return.

Bottom line? As you add content to your site, your VED should slowly increase. If it doesn't, check your navigation structure and then compare the traffic to different pages to find out what visitors like and don't like.

Reference Link:
http://blog.webanalyticsdemystified.com/weblog/2007/10/how-to-measure-visitor-engagement-redux.html

7. Web Viewing Volume (WVV)

Equation: WVV = P/T

Where P = number of Pages viewed by a unique visitor, and

T = Time period.

Description: Web Viewing Volume determines the number of pages viewed per given time period per visitor. In general, the more page views per time period, the more engaged the visitor is, assuming, of course, that pages are not heavily text-oriented.

Example: Visitor A stays on the site for 10 minutes. He views 38 different pages.

38/10 = 3.8 pages per minute. His WVV is 3.8 pages per minute.

To use WVV effectively, first consider the nature (and uniformity) or your pages. If your pages are long and content-heavy, low WVVs are understandable. For example, if each page contains 800-1,000 words of text, the WVV should be relatively long. If most pages contain brief text descriptions and photos, WVVs should be relatively short.

In general terms, multiple page views of relatively short duration means the visitor has found a number of pages of interest; he or she may return to those pages at a later date. (Of course, the opposite outcome may be true: Multiple page views of a short duration could mean the visitor is struggling to find interesting content. In those cases the average visitor will not look at more than four to five pages before moving on to another site.)

The key is to first consider the goal of your site. Are your pages intended to hold visitors for extended periods (lots of text, videos, or interactive content)? Use WVV to see if that strategy is working; if your WVV is high, it's not working. Or, do you want visitors to move quickly through your site to an intended destination (like a sale or a sign-up?) Use WVV to see if that strategy is working; if your WVV is low, visitors are getting "stuck" somewhere.

You can dig deeper by analyzing the ASL for each page, and make changes to either streamline or extend the visits to those pages.

Here's a quick example: You have eight pages on your site; each page contains a ten-minute video. In a perfect world your WVV would be .1 per minute, since each video takes ten minutes to watch. If your WVV is 1, that means the average visitor is only giving each video about a minute before moving on... either your content is poor or you're attracting the wrong visitors.

Reference link: http://www.jimnovo.com/metrics-definitions.htm

8. Average Traffic per Page (ATP)

Equation: ATP = TV/TP

Where TV = Total Visitors, and

TP = Total number of Pages.

Description: Average Traffic per Page calculates the average visits per page on a site-wide basis; ATP can then help determine which pages (or links) are popular with visitors and which are not.

Example: You had 1,000 visitors this month. Your site contains 20 pages.

1,000/20 = 50 pages per visitor. Your ATP is 50.

Like a few other metrics, ATP is directionally accurate. Used as in the example above, it provides an average for all the pages on your site; it does not yield page-specific data. But, ATP does give you a yardstick against which to compare the performance of each page.

For example, say your ATP is fifty, as in the example above. Now determine the traffic each page on your site received. Some pages, like your home page, may have received two hundred or more visitors; one may have only attracted ten visitors. If your average is fifty, then clearly the page that only attracted ten visitors is under-performing. Possibly that's by design; maybe it's your "About Us" page, and you don't expect many visitors to be interested in your bios. If it's a product page, then your average visitor isn't particularly interested in that page – you may want to change marketing tactics ... or you may not. That's a decision only you can make.

Reference link: http://www.jimnovo.com/metrics-definitions.htm

9. Average Number of Visits per Visitor (AVPV)

Equation: AVPV= V/UV

Where V = total number of Visits, and

UV = number of Unique visitors.

Description: Average Number of Visits per Visitor measures how many visitors return, and how many times they return, per a specified period of time. In general terms, the higher the average the more successfully you are engaging your visitors.

Example: Last month 4,000 total visitors landed on your site. 3,000 of those were unique visitors.

4,000/3,000 =1.33. Last month your AVPV was 1.33.

Is that a good number? Again, it depends (and it's a metric best evaluated over time). If you run a blog, 1.33 visits per visitor may be low; some major blogs can average ten, twenty, or more average visits per visitor. Or if you run a niche blog, your AVPV could be high because your content is highly relevant ... but only to a small group of people. (In other words, you don't have a lot of fans – but the fans you do have are very loyal.)

The key is to measure your AVPV over time. Adding relevant content on a frequent basis should increase your AVPV. But don't change too many variables at once: If you add a lot of content but also double your advertising, your AVPV may stay flat because you will attract a number of new site visitors who may not stay.

Also keep in mind the nature of your site. Say you sell products. If your product(s) requires a lot of thought on the part of buyers (in other words, you sell expensive items), expect a high AVPV as people come back again and again to think through the purchase. If you sell lower-priced impulse items, your AVPV should be low because visitors should come, look ... and buy. If you make money through advertising, a high AVPV indicates you have loyal visitors that advertisers may covet. If you provide customer support, hopefully your AVPV is low – visitors get their problems resolved once and for all and don't need to return.

In general, your AVPV should stay relatively flat if your site has been up for at least six to nine months and you haven't made major changes in marketing or content. If you make changes, evaluate the result and either go back to the drawing board or rinse and repeat!

Reference Link:
http://www.searchengineguide.com/manoj-jasra/measuring-visit.php

10. Heat Map Expectation (HME)

Equation: HME = Either what you did or didn't expect (see below)

Description: A heat map is a visual representation of visitor activity. Heat map tools provided by services like crazyegg.com let you see which links and items are more popular than others.

Example: See below.

Heat maps are fun visual tools. Basically it creates an "overlay" of a web page; the more frequently a link or other item has been clicked by visitors, the "hotter" that area appears. In seconds you can not only see what links are popular and which aren't – you can get a sense of how users interact with your site.

Why is that knowledge useful? Your assumption of what visitors do may be far removed from the reality of their behavior. You may be convinced the banner ad you placed at the upper right portion of your home page will result in hundreds of clicks, while in fact a small link located at the bottom left, pointing to the same page, has generated hundreds of clicks while your banner is largely ignored. In short, a heat map shows you whether your visitors click where you expect them – or want them – to click, and if not where they *do* click.

The result either validates or invalidates your expectation; either way, now you *know*.

There are a number of tools you can take advantage of. One is offered by crazyegg.com; a trial period is free. Or check out RobotReplay.com for a tool that generates a video of visitor behavior. You'll see mouse movements, clicks, keystrokes, and pages visited. Not only will you see what your visitors do, but you can see where they struggle or appear to become confused – and you can make changes to your site to create a better user experience. (You can especially monitor user behavior to see where visitors struggle – and as a result leave you without making a purchase – during the shopping and check-out process.)

Reference Link:
http://realtytimes.com/rtpages/20080207_boostsite.htm

11. Number of Clicks per Visitor (CPV)

Equation: CPV= CT/VT

Where CT = Total Clicks, and

VT = Total Visitors

Description: Clicks per Visitor identifies the difference between ad clicks and unique visitors based on those clicks. Typically used in pay-per-click campaigns, like Google AdWords, for billing purposes.

Example: You sell soccer equipment. A customer sees your AdWord ad at the top of a search result. They click the ad to visit your site. They scan the page briefly and leave. They check out a few of your competitors, determine you had the best price, and come back to your site through the AdWords ad. While they have clicked your ad twice, in Analytics terms they are only counted as one visitor to your site because they returned within minutes. Your total clicks are 2. Your total visitor count is 1.

$2/1 = 2$. You had 2 CPV.

And yes, in effect you paid twice for the same visitor.

While you would hope your CPV would never be higher than 1, in reality it almost always is. Many people will neglect to bookmark your site; they'll find you each time through an ad, especially if they're comparison shopping (and aren't concerned about your advertising spending). But, sometimes they will bookmark your site or remember the URL –in which case one click results in multiple visits and your CPV may drop below 1.

What can you do to maximize the efficiency of your ads and keep your CPV as low as possible? Create clear, easy to understand ads, target your market, and make it as easy as possible – and attractive – for buyers to buy the first time they visit your site. If your CPV gets out of hand, look for ways to improve the entire process.

Reference Link:
http://www.google.com/support/analytics/bin/answer.py?hl=en&answer=57164

12. New Visits Ratio (NVR)

Equation: NVR =V/T

Where V = number of new Visits, and

T = Time period.

Description: The New Visits Ratio helps you determine if your site is growing – or declining – in terms of new visitors.

Example: You've worked hard on SEO, and you're dabbling in a consistent amount of SEM, too. This month you had 3,000 new visitors; last month you had 2,500 visitors.

Your NVR has increased from 2,500 to 3,000.

Success! (As long as you keep it up.)

Since that evaluation was pretty simple, let's take it a step further. In advertising terms, most analytics measure visits and visitors. "Visits" refers to the total amount of activity on your site. "Visitors" are individual, well, *visitors*: If a visitor leaves your site and returns within thirty minutes, they are only counted as one *visitor* even though they have made another *visit*, which will be added to your total number of visits. If they return more than thirty minutes later, their return adds both an additional visitor *and* an additional visit to your total.

So let's see the concept in action. Say this month you had 10,000 visitors resulting in 20,000 visits. Your visit to visitor ratio is 2. Next month you spend more on advertising; you get 12,000 visitors, resulting in 22,000 visits. Now your visit to visitor ratio is 1.83. Your visit ratio decreased; which means your new visitor ratio increased, hopefully because your advertising successfully drew new visitors. (A fact you could also have determined by using the NVR, but now you also know those new visitors don't come back within thirty minutes as frequently as last month's group did. Does that knowledge help you? Maybe… maybe not.)

In short, the higher the NVR, the more successful you should be able to consider your SEO and SEM efforts. If your NVR doesn't increase, something's wrong.

Fix it!

Reference Link:
http://www.google.com/support/analytics/bin/answer.py?hl=en&answer=57164

13. Customer Retention Rate (CRR)

Equation: CRR = {C_E - C_N/C_S} X 100

Where C_N = number of New Customers acquired during the year, and

C_S = number of Customers at the Start of the year, and

C_E = number of Customers at the End of the year.

Description: Complicated? Don't worry – we'll make it simple. For now, the CRR is a way to measure how many customers you keep over the long term; your goal is to ensure your site and your services retain the maximum number of customers.

Example: We'll use round numbers to keep the math simple. You start the year with 100 customers. You pick up 20 new customers, but you lose 10 existing customers; at the end of the year you have 110 customers.

$110 - 20 = 90$; $90/100 = .9$; $.9 \times 100 = 90\%$. Your CRR for the year is 90%.

If you want to take the calculations further, your acquisition rate was 20%; you picked up 20 new customers to add to the 100 you had at the beginning of the year. The problem is you lost 10 along the way; as a result, your attrition rate was 10%. In all, though, you're up – well done!

Many business owners know their acquisition rate because getting new customers is fun. Relatively few know their attrition rate; losing customers is no fun. Tracking CRR helps you put both in perspective and measure your results over time. What can you do to improve CRR? Can you introduce new pricing schemes, new terms, new products and services? Or are you okay with losing a few customers if the remaining customers generate higher profit margins?

Either way your CRR provides a sense-check to customer satisfaction and your competitive position in the marketplace.

Reference Link:
http://www.searchengineguide.com/manoj-jasra/are-you-measuri.php

14. Bookmark to Visitor Ratio (BVR)

Equation: BVR = V_B/ V_T X 100

Where V_B = Visitors who Bookmark the site, and

V_T = Total number of Visitors.

Description: A visitor who bookmarks your site wants to return. The more successful your brand – and your content – the more visitors will bookmark your site.

Example: 100,000 people visited your site last month. (You lucky dog.) 3,500 bookmarked your site.

3,500/100,000 = .035, or 3.5%. Your BVR is 3.5%.

Hmmm … is that a good result? Tough to tell – most sites don't publicize their BVR, so there is little to benchmark against. (Plus I'm still trying to get over the fact you had 100,000 visitors last month.) Your best bet is to evaluate BVR over time, or in relation to a variable you change.

Say, for example, you add videos to your site. If your BVR increases, that's a sign visitors like the videos and want to come back for more. If your BVR doesn't increase and your total visitor count doesn't increase, the videos may have had no tangible effect on your site's appeal… unless, of course, you notice that sales have jumped or your DAP (Desired Action Percentage) increases. (Remember: No variable, and no metric, is an island.)

So make tweaks and see what happens; just make sure your BVR isn't the only metric you evaluate. While it's one handy way to gauge the perceived value of your site, it's certainly not the *only* way.

Reference Link: http://www.webpublicitee.com/Visitor-tracking/index.html

15. Shopping Cart Abandonment Rate (SCAR)

Equation: SCAR = SCA/SCR X 100

Where SCA = number of Shopping Carts Abandoned, and

SCR = number of Shopping Carts Created.

Description: The Shopping Cart Abandonment Rate measures how many visitors add items to a shopping cart but never complete the actual purchase.

Example: You run an e-commerce site and last month 500 site visitors created and/or added items to a shopping cart. 400 completed the purchase; 100 did not.

100/500 = .2, or 20%. 20% of your customers left their shopping cart "in the aisle" and "walked" away.

SCAR is a useful way to measure your online sales efforts. Sadly, some customers will create a cart with no intention of making a purchase. (That's why, like with most metrics, evaluating SCAR over time is useful; you'll develop a good sense of your "normal" abandonment rate, and can work hard at decreasing the number of visitors who abandon their carts for some other reason.) Your goal is to make changes to help real customers complete their purchase. Possibly you need better product descriptions, photos, product specifications, installation instructions … anything to make a customer feel more comfortable about the purchase.

Or maybe they bail for a more basic reason: Possibly your prices aren't competitive and a comparison shopper finds a better deal and never comes back. (In the process, leaving behind a trail of abandoned shopping carts across the ecommerce landscape.)

Try this: Have a few friends work through your shopping process. You know the process inside-out; you won't make mistakes or get frustrated. But they might – and you might uncover problems you can eliminate that will decrease your SCAR. Or take a look at how many steps are required to find a product, add it to a shopping cart, and move on to the checkout stage. Most visitors will mentally compare your process to the ones used by major online marketers like Amazon.com; if your process is more difficult or cumbersome, they may quickly get frustrated and leave.

And if that's not the problem, take positive steps. Promote your return and exchange policies. Post security icons. Include some brief privacy language near customer data entry fields. Help the customer feel you're the solution to their needs – and all other variables remaining equal, your SCAR will decrease.

Reference Link: http://www.spectruminc.com/website-analytics/visitor-behavior.aspx

16. Next Page Request Ratio (NPRR)

Equation: NPRR = V_{NP} / V_T X 100

Where V_{NP} = Number of Visitors who made a Next Page request, and

V_T = Total number of Visitors.

Description: The Next Page Request Ratio measures the rate at which visitors click to visit a subsequent (internal) page.

Example: Let's keep this one simple. You have a home page with one link. 100 people visit your home page this month. You've created an incredible call to action and 80 people click the link to go to the subsequent page.

80/100 = .8, or 80%. Your NPRR is 80%.

The NPRR is designed to measure the efficiency of internal links. The higher your NPRR, the more attractive those links – whether text links, banners, calls to action, shopping cart adds, etc – and thus the more effective your site.

But all links are not created equal. If you have a number of navigation links and one "call to action" link on the same page, you don't mind if visitors ignore the navigation links in favor of the "call to action" link. If the navigation links are more popular, that's okay too – as long as visitors eventually heed your call to action. (Maybe they just needed a little more information before they took the next step?)

The key is to ensure your navigation structure, text, and link-naming conventions make the next steps obvious. For example, don't hide your "next page" link; make it easy for readers to find. Don't hide the submission box for the free report you'll send – make it easy to find. Lead your visitors – don't let them stumble around blindly. Think of it this way: Your links are like miniature advertisements – make sure important links clearly demonstrate the value a visitor will receive by clicking through.

Reference Link:
http://www.streetdirectory.com/travel_guide/10020/web_development/metrics_matter.html

17. Average Number of Visits per Subscriber (AVS)

Equation: AVS = V/S

Where V = number of Visits, and

       S = number of Subscribers.

AV_S = Number of visits paid by subscribers, on an average basis.

Description: Average Visits per Subscriber measures, at least in part, the use and value subscribers find in a website. AVS takes the concept of RVI (Repeat Visitor Index) to the next level, measuring the activity of an incredibly important set of visitors – your subscribers. The higher the AVS, the higher the satisfaction of your subscribers … and the more likely they will remain subscribers.

Example: You have 400 subscribers to your marketing collateral service; only the subscribers have access to exclusive templates and how-to guides. In total your subscribers visited the site 3,000 times this month.

3,000/400 = 7.5. You average 7.5 AVS per month.

Good result? Maybe – but always strive to take your AVS to a higher level. The more times a subscriber visits, the more likely they are to be satisfied with your services, and the more opportunities you'll get to provide additional (hopefully paid) products and services.

In general terms, paid subscribers tend to generate higher AVS figures; they have a vested interest in returning (at least until they cancel their subscription). Free subscribers have little or no reason to return unless the site provides value; AVS rates will accordingly be much lower. Benchmark figures are difficult to come by. Measure your progress over time to gauge the effectiveness of your efforts.

For example, say your AVS is 10. You're happy with that number, but you'd like it to improve; currently you average two add-on sales per one hundred subscribers per month. You hope that increasing your AVS will increase your opportunities to market to subscribers and generate a higher rate of add-on sales. You add video content and partner with another website to offer additional content. Your AVS increases to 15, and your add-on sales double on a monthly basis.

Worth it? As long as any additional cost you incur is outweighed by additional sales revenue, absolutely!

Either way, AVS helps you know if your subscribers are happy; keep your finger on the AVS pulse.

18. Positive Feedback Ratio (PFR)

Equation: PFR = (PF / TF) X 100

Where PF = Positive Feedback, and

TF = Total Feedback.

Description: First a quick note. Feedback can be formal feedback, like a comment or survey result. Or "feedback" can be an action or outcome. (More in a moment.) In either instance, the Positive Feedback Ratio is the ratio of positive responses to total responses.

Example: You conduct a survey about a new product. 100 people respond; 60 respond in a manner you characterize as "positive" (for instance, they either prefer or strongly prefer your product to other similar products).

60/100 = .6, or 60%. Your Positive Feedback Ratio is 60%.

Or take another example: You create two distinct web pages, both designed to sell the same product. 100 people visit Page A, and out of those 100 visitors, 20 buy the product. The PFR for Page A is 20%. 100 people visit

Page B and 25 buy the product. The PFR for Page B is 25%. Page B is the winner in this little competition; ditch Page A and use Page B.

In the second example we used A/B testing to determine the "winning" PFR. (A/B testing is also sometimes called "split testing"). The product is not the variable; the variable is the method used to sell the product. PFR testing allows you to determine which type of advertising, sales techniques, or page design (among other variables) most effectively sells your product.

Split testing is also commonly used to evaluate different types of advertising. Say you are running a Google AdWords campaign; many advertisers try variations of copy to see which generates the highest click through rates (and the greatest sales.) In that instance, each ad would generate a different PFR; all other factors being equal, the highest PFR wins.

PFR is most useful when you control as many variables as possible; that way you know which factor made the difference. Feel free to change page titles, images, headlines, page element placement, return policies... changes that generate higher PFR are keepers; throw out the duds and keep moving forward.

Reference Link:
http://en.wikipedia.org/wiki/A/B_testing

19. Cart Checkout Ratio (CCR)

Equation: CCR =CA/C X 100

Where CA = Checkout Abandoned, and

C = Checkouts.

Description: The Cart Checkout Ratio is similar to the SCAR metric (Shopping Cart Abandonment Rate). CCR helps measure the number of checkout processes that were abandoned, not the number of shopping carts abandoned. The result helps evaluate drawbacks in the checkout process that may cause checkout abandonment.

Example: You sell soccer supplies ... no, wait, you've gone upscale; now you sell golf equipment. You get 10,000 visitors per month and 500 of those visitors create shopping carts. 450 of those visitors initiated the checkout process by clicking the "Checkout Now" button. Out of those 450 people, only 430 completed their purchase; 20 abandoned prematurely.

20/450 = .044, or 4.4%. Your CCR is 4.4%; those visitors initiated the checkout process but abandoned the process prior to sale completion.

Realistically speaking your CCR should be significantly lower than your SCAR. Shopping cart abandonment is fairly common; once a visitor clicks "Checkout Now," they have basically committed to the purchase unless you make the checkout process difficult. Typically no more than three pages are required; take whatever time is necessary to test and optimize those pages so you lose as few sales as possible. If you have more pages, make them easy to use – and consider testing a few changes to the process to determine if your CCR is positively affected.

Common causes of CCR include insufficient payment options, a cumbersome data entry interface, and "special offers" that interrupt (and potentially irritate) a customer who has almost reached the finish line. Shipping charges can be another roadblock; pre-sell customers by making shipping rates available before the actual checkout process begins. Out of stock warnings made after credit card info has been entered can also chase customers away at the last moment.

Other options include adding pictures of the items to the cart basket; research shows conversions increase by up to 10% when pictures are included. Include a "progress meter" on the page to let the customer know where they stand in the checkout process. And make it easy to edit the shopping cart even when the checkout process has started; you may lose one part of the sale, but you won't lose the entire sale because you force the customer to start over.

Reference Link: http://www.clickz.com/2245891

20. Percentage of Indexed Pages (PIP)

Equation: PIP = (IP / TP) X 100

Where IP = Number of Indexed Pages

TP = Total number of Pages on the website

Description: The Percentage of Indexed Pages determines the ratio of pages that have been found and indexed by search engines. The larger the ratio, the more pages have been indexed – and the more successful the site is from a SEO perspective.

Example: Your site contains 1,000 separate pages. (You've obviously been busy.) Out of those 1,000 pages, only 100 have been indexed by Google.

100/1,000 = .1, or 10%. Your PIP is 10%.

The good news is 100 of your pages are indexed; the bad news is Google is basically ignoring your other 900 pages. If Google ignores those pages, then visitors won't find those pages through a Google search. (If a web page falls in the forest and no one is there to hear it, does it make a sound?)

Determining how many pages have been indexed is simple. Search with Google using the term "site:(yoursite).com." So, if you own Yahoo! (and please call me if you do), Google the term site:www.yahoo.com and you'll see all the pages that have been spidered by Google.

If your PIP is low, check for obvious problems: Broken links, non-text links, cumbersome dynamic URLs … and create a site map to make the process easier for the spiders. If those efforts don't work, bring in an SEO specialist. Your goal should be to have all pages indexed – or at least the ones you want to be indexed. (You may not want sensitive pages crawled, but that begs a question: Why waste time having any pages you don't want visitors to find?)

Reference Link:
http://www.seoptimise.com/blog/2008/08/33-website-success-metrics-instead-of-rankings-google-pagerank-and-traffic.html

21. Alexa Rank (AR)

Equation: AR = Alexa-calculated traffic Rank

Description: Alexa.com is a website ranking and analysis service that provides statistics regarding website traffic. In general terms, the lower your Alexa rank, the more heavily visited your site. (As of this writing, Google is

Alexa's top-ranked site, followed closely by Yahoo and YouTube.)

Example: You want a sense of how your website stacks up against the competition. You go to Alexa.com and enter your site; if you're lucky your site will rank in the top 100,000 and you'll see additional data. If it doesn't, you'll get a numerical ranking. (Don't be surprised if your site ranks in the hundreds of thousands.) For fun, try entering your competitors to see how they rank.

You may be tempted to focus on boosting your Alexa rank. (After all, who wants to rank in the hundreds of thousands at *anything*?)

Before you do, think about the nature of your business first. If you've monetized your website through advertising, a strong Alexa rank can definitely help you convince advertisers or ad networks that your site gets a lot of visitors, which will increase your bargaining power. (Online ad networks like Sponsored Reviews and Text Link Ads use Alexa rankings to help determine your site's ad selling strength.)

If you don't sell advertising on your site, your Alexa ranking is a lot less important. Chase a higher ranking if you want, but recognize the value of doing so has more to do with ego and less with site performance. The simplest way is to install the Alexa Toolbar on your site, but there are a number of additional techniques you can also try.

22. Google Page Rank (PR)

Equation: PR = Page Rank assigned by Google

Description: Page Rank is a numerical value denoting Google's evaluation of the relative importance of a particular web page. Rankings range from "No Page Rank Information Available" to a Page Rank of 10. Page Ranks over 6 are rarely awarded; the average website ranks between 2 and 4.

Example: Your home page has a Page Rank of 4 on a scale of 1 to 10. What does that mean? The answer is … it depends.

Determining Page Rank is easy; install the Google Toolbar on your browser, and you can see the Page Rank of any page. If you don't want to install the toolbar, search using the phrase "page rank" and you'll find a variety of free online tools. (The tradeoff is you'll have to enter URLs individually, but that way you will avoid having the Google Toolbar on your browser.)

According to Google, "Page Rank relies on the uniquely democratic nature of the web by using its vast link structure as an indicator of an individual page's value. In essence, Google interprets a link from page A to page B as a vote, by page A, for page B. But, Google looks at more than the sheer volume of votes or links a page receives; it also analyzes the page that casts the vote. Votes cast by pages that are themselves "important" weigh more heavily and help to make other pages 'important.'"

Keep in mind Page Rank is not the sole measure of your site's importance. For example, your site can have a low Page Rank yet rank highly for specific keywords. Traffic is all-important; if your site draws targeted traffic and converts visitors to buyers at a solid rate, for example, your Page Rank doesn't matter. Page Rank is just one indication of the success of your SEO efforts.

Reference Link: http://en.wikipedia.org/wiki/PageRank

23. Google Cache Interval (GCI)

Equation: GCI = Google Cache date Interval

Description: As pages are crawled, Google creates a cache of those pages. The cache is refreshed each time pages are crawled. The shorter the elapsed time between cache dates, the more frequently Google indexes the site and the more "important" Google considers the site. Cache dates greater than one month can indicate the site is no longer being indexed, or that Google sees the site as relatively unimportant.

Example: Your site has a cache date of March 1. You check back frequently, and you find a new Cache Date of March 8. Your GCI is 7 days.

GCI is another tool, like Page Rank, you can use to determine where your site ranks with Google. The more frequently your site is cached, the quicker new content appears in search results. (Although the Google bot may visit more frequently – even if your pages aren't cached every time, the bot will often visit once a day, even on small sites.) You can decrease your GCI by adding fresh content, getting back links ... in effect, by performing standard SEO techniques.

Reference Link:

http://www.seoptimise.com/blog/2008/08/33-website-success-metrics-instead-of-rankings-google-pagerank-and-traffic.html

24. Social Media Submissions (SMS)

Equation: SMS = Submissions to Social Media sites

Description: Social media submissions to sites like Digg, Slashdot, Reddit, et al can dramatically improve website traffic. Mentions on niche sites can yield targeted traffic. SMS measures those submissions.

Example: You write a story called "Ten Indications the World Was Created Yesterday" (or something much more relevant and creative). Visitors read your story, like it, and submit the page to a social media site like Digg.com. Other visitors submit the page to StumbleUpon or Reddit.

Enough submissions and "votes" and your traffic may jump exponentially – at least in the short-term.

Keep in mind the impact, in terms of traffic, of social media submissions tends to be brief: Visitors see the link, click to your site, possibly stick around … and then move on. (But some will return if they like what they see.)

So, use SMS as an indication of the success of new content you create, at least in social media terms. If you write a new article and SMS is high, you've done well; if your SMS doesn't budge, revisit your content or how you're attempting to get the word out.

Just remember: SMS helps you evaluate the relative success, in social media terms, of a particular article or page; the next metric helps you evaluate your overall success in social media.

Reference Link:
http://www.seoptimise.com/blog/2008/08/33-website-success-metrics-instead-of-rankings-google-pagerank-and-traffic.html

25. Social News Submission Rate (SNSR)

Equation: NSR = NS/T

Where NS = Number of social media news Submissions for site elements, and

$\qquad$ T = Time.

Description: Unlike SMS, which measures the number of submissions for a specific piece of content, Social News Submission Rate evaluates the success of your site, in social media terms, over a specified time period. The higher the rate of submissions, the more relevant and valuable social media users find your site.

Example: You steadily and consistently create new content; each month you post ten new articles and two new videos on your site. Over the course of the month various pages on your site are submitted 14 times to social media sites like Digg and Reddit.

14/ 1 (month) = 14 per month; your Social News Submission Rate is 14 per month.

If site content is submitted sixteen times next month, your SNSR is 16 per month. It could be more visitors in total are finding your site, which yields more total opportunities to be submitted to social networking sites. Or, the new content you continue to develop could be more relevant to your visitors.

You'll never know for sure, but an easy way to tell if the increase is simply due to an increase in visitors is to divide your submissions by your total visitors for the time period. For example, say last month you had 1,000 visitors and you received 50 social news submissions; your visitors submit you at a 5% rate – 5% of your visitors submit your content to a social networking site. If this month you have 1,100 visitors and you receive 60 submissions, your rate is 5.45%. The number of total visitors increased, but your submission per visitor rate is up. In general terms, it sounds like your content is increasing in appeal.

Both social news metrics are important. SMS is a great way to evaluate the effectiveness of a particular piece of content – if you tend to average 5 "Diggs" per article, and a new article yielded 20 "Diggs," take a closer look at that article. What makes it stand out? The headline? Content? Where it appeared on your site? Whatever the factors – duplicate them next time on a new article!

SNSR is also helpful in a more general, overall sense. Visitors hopefully browse a variety of content. As they do, they may submit a variety of pages to social media sites. If your SNSR increases, that's a great sign that your site appeal is increasing to the average visitor. One great article may receive a ton of submissions and skew the numbers for one month, but over time you'll see whether your site is increasing or decreasing in popularity, at least in social media terms.

Reference Link:

http://www.seoptimise.com/blog/2008/08/33-website-success-metrics-instead-of-rankings-google-pagerank-and-traffic.html

26. Keyword Visibility Ratio (KVR)

Equation: KVR = (NK/TK) X 100

Where NK = Number of Keywords appearing in first ten positions, and

TK = Total targeted Keywords.

Description: Keyword Visibility Ratio indicates the percentage of your keywords that rank highly in search engine results. In essence, KVR is an indication of the success (or failure) of your overall SEO efforts.

Example: You sell candy. You try to rank well for a number of keywords: taffy, hard candy, chocolate, chewing gum ... in all you developed a list of 200 targeted keywords. You check each keyword in the search rankings, and out of the 200 you submit, 40 appear in the top ten.

40/200 = .2, or 20%. Your KVR is 20%.

Ads are an effective – if sometimes costly – way to drive traffic. Natural search engine traffic is free ... but you only get that traffic if your keywords are highly ranked. Keywords ranking in the top ten significantly out-perform lower-ranked keywords. (In fact, if your site shows up on the third or fourth page of the results, your site might as well be in Siberia. (Few searchers look past the first page.)

Collect search result data from Google and Yahoo! Feel free to try other search engines if you like, but keep in mind Google and Yahoo! account for the vast majority of search traffic.

Once you know your KVR, your next step is to improve it. New customers are looking for you – make it easy for them to find you!

Reference Link: http://www.search-visibility.com/

27. Brand Index (BI)

Equation: BI = (BS/TV) X 100

Where BS = visits originating from Brand Searches, and

TV = Total Visits

Description: Brand Index calculates the percentage of total site visits that were initiated based on an external search for a "branded" term. A branded term is a term you feel is unique to or indicative of your site content. (For example, a branded term could be your name or the name of your product or company.)

Example: Last month you had 1,000 site visitors. You sell a specific type of exercise equipment, and 150 of those visitors found your site by searching for the name of that equipment.

150/1,000 = .15, or 15%. Your Brand Index for that term is 15%.

Keep in mind you can have a number of branded terms and you can calculate a Brand Index for each. And, while in most cases visitors will arrive through a search engine, if your branded term is the same as your URL, anyone typing your URL to visit your site can certainly be counted as a "branded visitor."

At a basic level, Brand Index can give you a sense of the effectiveness of your marketing efforts, especially if your goal is to raise awareness of your company, your name, your products, etc. (Think of it this way: Say you developed and sell "Rocket Golf Clubs." "Rocket Golf Clubs could be a branded term; visitors who arrive after searching for "rocket golf clubs" count towards your BI; visitors who arrive after searching for "golf club" or "golf equipment" do not – they are searching for a general product rather than your specific product. So if, over time, your BI increases, that's a sign your overall marketing efforts are paying off.

Also keep in mind a visitor who arrives from a pay-per-click ad can also be counted as a branded visitor ... as long as he or she searched for the branded term in the first place before clicking your ad. A visitor who searched for "golf clubs" and saw (and clicked) your ad for Rocket Golf Clubs is not a branded visitor; a visitor who searched for "Rocket Golf Clubs" and clicked your ad, instead of a natural search result, is a branded visitor.

Let's look at a quick example. Say your site – and your marketing – focuses on four branded terms. You add up the BIs for each term and find that 90% of your visitors come to the site due to searching for those terms. Your marketing – at least from a branded term awareness point of view – is very successful. On the other hand, if the total of your BIs is low, from an awareness point of view your marketing efforts are not paying off; the search traffic you receive is of the "long tail" variety.

Reference Link:
http://blog.webanalyticsdemystified.com/weblog/2007/10/how-to-measure-visitor-engagement-redux.html

28. Traffic Yield Ratio (TYR)

Equation: TYR = PT/TP X 100

Where PT = Pages that yield Traffic, and

TP = Total Pages.

Description: Traffic Yield can be evaluated in a number of ways. One method is to determine the percentage of site pages that yield traffic. Another is to compare the traffic for a particular page against average traffic for all site pages. (We'll look at both.)

Example 1: Your site has 200 total pages. Of those 200 pages, 50 generated traffic from visitors last month.

50/200 = .2, or 20%. Your TYR is 20%. (In terms of pages that generate traffic.)

Example 2: Your site received 1,000 visitors last month. You have 200 pages. The average page yielded 5 visitors per month. (Understanding that some pages receive no traffic, and some receive dozens of visitors – we've just determined an average.) But, one page yielded 40 visitors; it greatly exceeds the average. Out of 200 pages, it accounted for 4% of all visitors (40 / 200). It's a highly successful page.

TYR helps you differentiate between useful pages and non-useful pages, at least in terms of yielding traffic. (It could be that a page yields very little traffic, and that's okay; for example, few people look at the Terms & Conditions or Privacy Policy pages, but almost every site needs them.) The key is to look critically at your most important pages: Your home page, major landing pages, product pages, pages you've worked hard to optimize, and evaluate their performance against the rest of the site.

In a perfect world, all pages will yield traffic (except, hopefully, not your Returns and Exchanges page), but in real terms you didn't create all pages equally. TYR helps you evaluate how your most important pages are doing and target under-performing pages in need of improvement.

Reference Link: N/A

29. Onsite Search Session Ratio (OSSR)

Equation: OSSR = SS/TS X 100

Where SS = onsite Search Sessions, and

TS = Total Sessions.

Description: The Onsite Search Session Ratio determines the frequency with which visitors use your on-site search tools to navigate your site.

Example: Last month you had 5,000 visitors. 200 of those visitors utilized your on-site search tool to find a particular page or product.

825/5,000 = .165, or 16.5%. Your OSSR for the month was 16.5%.

Why is OSSR important? Once they reach your site, a percentage of visitors will prefer to use on-site search tools rather than your navigation structure and other content cues (like headings, drop-down menus, etc.) Others do not prefer to search on-site, but are left with no choice if they find it difficult to navigate your site. And as a by-product of the process, by collecting on-site search data you can get clues about what your visitors are interested in – and what they were motivated to reach but struggled to find.

First look at your site. If you provide massive amounts of content, on-site search may be the best way for visitors to find what they're looking for; instead of creating complicated navigation structures or link-intensive pages, you could feature on-site searching prominently on your pages. Then, if your OSSR rate increases, you'll know those efforts paid off.

On the other hand, if your site has relatively little content, a high OSSR could indicate your site is poorly laid out and difficult to navigate. Lowering your OSSR means visitors more readily find what they're looking for – and overall site performance should improve.

Bottom line: Determine your goals for your site, and then use OSSR to determine whether you're making progress towards those goals.

Reference Link: http://www.stratigent.com/web-sight-newsletter/web-analytics-newsletter-archive/tracking-onsite-search/default.html

30. Number of Google Blog Search Links (GBL)

Equation: GBL = Total number of Google Blog search Links for a site

Description: Google Blog Search is a search engine that focuses on indexing blogs. Using Blog search, you can determine how many inbound links your site receives from other websites; the result is an indication of your website's popularity among the blogging community.

Example: Your website has been linked to 30 links by bloggers. Your GBL is 30.

Simple? Sure – but it's a good indication of the popularity of your site among bloggers. Tracking your GBL on a monthly basis will also show whether your site is increasing or decreasing in popularity; if bloggers are a target audience, knowing your popularity within that community is critical.

Determining your GBL is easy. Go to blogsearch.google.com. Enter the url of your site in the search bar. The result shows all your inbound links from blog sites. (Not only can you see the total number of links, you can see exactly who is linking to you.)

For fun, you can check out your competitors or others in your industry; you'll get a sense of how they're doing and you might identify influential bloggers you wish to curry favor with.

Reference Link:
http://www.seoptimise.com/blog/2008/08/33-website-success-metrics-instead-of-rankings-google-pagerank-and-traffic.html

Category: Advertising Performance

31. Conversion Rate (CR)

Equation: CR = VC/TV X 100

Where VC = Visitors Converted, and

TV = Total Visitors.

Description: Conversion Rate measures the percentage of people who took a particular action compared to the total number of people who could have taken that action. (Typically the action is a purchase, but could also be a sign-up, request for more information, download a demo, etc. How "conversion" is defined depends on your original goal.) For example, this metric measures the extent to which an advertising program was successful in converting visitors into customers.

Example: You send an e-mail to each of the 1,500 people on your mailing list about a new promotion. 185 of those people click the link in your e-mail to go to your website to learn more about the offer.

185/1500 = .123, or 12.3%. Out of your entire mailing list, 12.3% responded to the offer, or were "converted."

Keep in mind "converted" can mean different things. In the example above, your goal was to get people on your mailing list to come to your website and check out your promotion. Since that was your goal, or your point of action, everyone who came to your website as a result of the e-mail is considered a conversion.

But, if your goal was to actually *sell* the product, the people who visited weren't converted. If 32 people actually bought the product, your CR was a much lower 2.1% (32/1,500).

CR is important because it measures the effectiveness of a particular action. If you send out 1,000 postcards and 32 people call your 800 number (and having customers call the number was your goal), then your conversion rate was 3.2%. If you add a newsletter sign-up box to your home page, and 1,500 out of the 200,000 visitors to that page sign up for the newsletter, your CR is .75%.

Some people measure "take rate" separately from Conversion Rate. Take rate refers to the percentage of visitors who took interest in an action but did not actually follow through with that action. Say you include a link for downloading a white paper on your home page; clicking the link leads to a separate page with download instructions, etc. Visitors who click the link to go to the download page count towards your take rate. Some will not actually download the white paper; only those who do are counted towards your conversion rate. So, if out of 1,000 people, 55 go to the download page, the take rate is 5.5%. If 35 download the white paper, the CR is 3.5% (out of all the people who clicked the original link).

If you want, you could compare conversions to "takers." Out of 55 "takers," 35 downloaded the white paper, for a CR of 63%. That means 63% of visitors to the download page followed through with the download, or were converted. Now you know two things: You know the rate at which visitors respond to the link on your home page, and you know the rate at which visitors follow through with the download once they reach the download page.

Your goal is obviously to increase all your Conversion Rates, whether through streamlining processes, targeting your marketing more effectively, or removing obstacles to the desired point of action.

Reference link:
http://www.conversionchronicles.com/Know_These_Thre e_Performance_Metrics_to_Increase_Website_Sales.html

32. Cost per Action (CPA)

Equation: CPA = ACI/TCA

Where ACI = Advertising Cost Incurred, and

TCA = Total Completed Actions.

Description: Cost per Action measures the amount spent to generate a single desired action to determine the efficiency of an advertising strategy or technique. CPA can be used to measure the effectiveness of an advertising campaign or to determine the actual charge for an advertising campaign.

Example #1: You send an e-mail to your mailing list describing a special offer. Design, layout, and system costs total $500. 780 people respond to the mailer and purchase your product.

$500 / 780 = .64. Your CPA was .64.

Example #2: You place banner ads on a website. Instead of being billed at a flat rate for a monthly period, or by impression (meaning the total number of visitors to that site), you agree to be charged $1 for every person who clicks the banner to visit your site. 4,000 people click the banner ad. In this instance, the math is easy; the CPA is already set at $1, so you are charged $4,000.

CPA is a performance based metric. If you advertise on someone else's site, they take the risk for running the ad – if no one clicks the ad, you owe no money. Pay-per-click is the most common form of CPA advertising; if you are running an AdWords campaign and no one clicks your ads, you owe Google no money. You are only charged when a customer takes action and clicks your ad.

CPA also helps you evaluate your cost of sales. If you run performance-based advertising campaigns (like banner ads or pay-per-click advertising) then your CPA is already set; you know the cost of acquiring a new visitor or customer. If you're running a non performance-based campaign, CPA helps you determine the true cost of each sale. Say you are charged $400 to place a banner ad on a site for a month. You make 20 sales as the result of that ad. Your CPA is $20. If you make 40 sales, your CPA falls to $40.

In either case, you know exactly how much acquiring the customer cost. Compare that cost to other forms of advertising to find the most efficient way to reach new customers. After all, a new customer is great – but only if acquiring that customer lets you make a profit.

Refernce link:

http://www.marketingterms.com/dictionary/cost_per_action/

33. Cost-Benefit Ratio (CBR)

Equation: CBR = S/CI

Where S = Sales, and

CI = Costs Incurred.

Description: In this case, the Cost-Benefit Ratio refers to measuring the performance of a particular advertising campaign.

Example: You spend $5,000 on advertising, and generate $28,000 as a result of that advertising.

$28,000/$5,000 = $5.6. Your CBR is $5.6 per $1 spent on advertising.

Keep in mind your CBR does not measure profitability; it's simply a handy way to compare different advertising campaigns. (CBR is like the cousin of Cost Per Action.) If the price of your product stays the same, CBR lets you measure the effectiveness of different campaigns so you compare apples to apples. For example, say you spent $3,000 on Campaign A, and the result was $20,000 in sales. You also spent $4,000 on Campaign B and got $25,000 in sales. You delivered a different message in each campaign; so which campaign performed better? After all, Campaign B brought in more total dollars.

Let's compare them. The CBR for Campaign A is $6.66 ($20,000/$3,000.) The CBR for Campaign B is $6.25 ($25,000/$4,000.) While Campaign B brought in more sales, the CBR is lower – that means your ad spending was less efficient. It is very possible that spending more on Campaign A would have yielded a higher rate of sales; if your CBR remains constant, spending $4,000 on Campaign A should result in $26,640 in sales rather than the $25,000 in sales you received from running Campaign B.

Reference Link: http://en.wikipedia.org/wiki/Benefit-cost_ratio

34. Value Of a Buyer (VOB)

Equation: VOB= ASP X GP

Where ASP = Average Sale Price, and

GP = Gross Profit (as a percentage of sales).

Description: Value of a Buyer calculates the average gross profit (after advertising costs) earned from a sale; the result helps you understand how effectively your advertising and web strategies turns visitors into profitable customers.

Example: You sell e-books; the average customer purchases $25 in e-books. (Some buy two, some buy one, some buy four, etc. In aggregate, the average customer spends $25.) Your gross profit margin (GPM) on e-books is 40%, meaning you make a 40% profit on each sale.

$25 X 40% = $10. Your VOB is $10; each buyer generates an average of $10 in gross profits.

VOB is interesting in itself, but it is a metric best used in comparison to metrics like Cost Per Action (CPA). Say your CPA for the example above is $3; if that's the case, you're making money on your e-books because your VOB is $10. (Getting the visitor cost $3, but in return you made $10 in gross profits.) If your CPA is higher than your VOB, you're losing money on every visitor you acquire through that form of advertising – time to make adjustments to your advertising campaign or find ways to increase your conversion rate so even more visitors become buyers.

Reference Link:

http://www.conversionchronicles.com/Know_These_Thre e_Performance_Metrics_to_Increase_Website_Sales.html

35. Sales Per Visit (SPV)

Equation: SPV=SP/NV X 100

Where SP = Total Sales, and

NV = Number of Visits.

Description: Sales Per Visit measures how effectively site visitors are converted into sales.

Example: You get 7,500 visitors to your site this month (from natural searches, returning visitors, advertising … in other words, from all sources.) You sell one product, and 420 of those visitors purchase your product.

420/7500 = .056, or 5.6%. 5.6% of your visitors purchase a product.

SPV doesn't just measure advertising effectiveness (if you're even running advertising). It measures how effectively your site – and your individual pages – turns visitors into actual customers. Keep in mind a "customer" and a "sale" can mean many things: You may sell a product, or you may just want newsletter sign-ups, or requests for more information ... a "sale" occurs when a "customer" takes the action you want them to take.

If you sell a product and improve SPV, you make more money. If your goal is to spread brand awareness by providing free reports, when SPV increases brand awareness increases.

You can also measure SPV using dollar amounts. Say you get 1,000 visitors, and your average sale is $40.25. $40.25/1,000 = .04; your SPV is 4 cents. If you find ways to increase your average sales – like by attracting more traffic more interested in a variety of your products or by attracting traffic interested in your higher-priced products – then your SPV will increase.

Reference Link: http://www.ezineads.info/frequently-asked-questions

36. Click Through Rate (CTR)

Equation: CTR= NC/AI

Where NC = Number of Clicks, and

AI = Number of Impressions.

Description: Click Through Rate measures the percentage of people that click on an ad compared to the total number of times the ad could have been seen ("impressions").

Example: You run an AdWords campaign for one keyword. Your ad is displayed on 40,000 web pages this week. 420 people click your ad to visit your website.

620/40,000 = .0155, or 1.55%. Your CTR is 1.55%.

I intentionally used an example with a low CTR because, in most cases, CTRs tend to be low. For one, many people never click on ads. And, your ad may not be particularly relevant to everyone who searched using a particular keyword. (For example, if your keyword is "candy" but your ad refers to "chocolate taffy candy," many people may see your ad but only chocolate taffy lovers will be interested, and only a portion of *those* people will click through.)

As a result, a CTR of 2% or higher is considered to be a fairly good result, unless your keyword is highly specialized – in that case you'd expect a higher CTR. In general terms, the broader the appeal of your keyword, the lower your CTR will be; you're casting a really wide net that may only catch a few of the right type of fish.

Also keep in mind that CTR is usually calculated by measuring the number of clicks and the number of impressions. If the same person clicks an ad multiple times, each click is considered a click. CTR is usually not measured by the number of visitors against the number of impressions.

Here's a quick example: One person sees an ad 100 times; if he clicks the ad 4 times, the CTR is 4%. If CTR is measured by the number of visitors, the CTR is 1%.

CTR can be improved by changing the wording of ads, improving the visibility of ads, better targeting your marketing so more impressions are seen by people who are interested in your products and services ... you get the idea. A/B testing (as explained in Positive Feedback Ratio, or PFR) is a great way to compare different ads or different ad placements to determine how to improve your click through rates.

Reference Link: http://en.wikipedia.org/wiki/Click-through_rate

37. Clicks Per Thousand (CPM)

Equation: CPM =EC/I X 1000

Where EC = Effective Clicks, and

I = Impressions.

Description: Clicks Per Thousand measures the percentage of clicks received per thousand impressions. CPM is often used to evaluate the effectiveness of advertising campaigns. (The M in CPM stands for Thousand.)

Example: Your banner ad is delivered 3,750 times (impressions.) 84 people click the ad to visit your website.

84/3750 = .0224; .0224 X 1000 = 22.4 Clicks Per Thousand.

Why not just say your click rate was 2.2% (84/3750)? While it's accurate, the click rate doesn't "normalize" performance, and doesn't account for the fact the advertiser may be able to deliver significantly more impressions than you expect. By using CPM, you can spend a pre-determined amount based on gross impressions.

Think of it this way: You decide to run a banner ad on the Yahoo! home page. (Hopefully you have deep pockets.) You will run the ad for one day. How many impressions will Yahoo! deliver? It's hard to tell – their traffic varies. It could be 2 million, it could be 2.5 million ... so instead of pricing their advertising by the time period, they price advertising by CPM. If your CPM is $20, and Yahoo! delivers 1 million total impressions, you are charged $20,000. If Yahoo! delivered 1.5 million total impressions, you are charged $30,000.

CPM is also a useful tool for determining what you will charge people who advertise on your site. The higher the CPM, the more money you make. If you deliver a targeted audience (for example, your blog is about golf, and a golf club manufacturer wants to run an ad on your site), then you're the CPM you charge can be relatively high; if your audience is fragmented, the CPM will likely be lower –

unless the advertiser has a product that is of broad interest to a wide variety of people.

Keep in mind that ad campaigns based on CPM are not performance-based (other than the fact you are charged more if the website running your ad can attract more visitors.) Just because people *see* your ad doesn't mean they will click through to your website. CPM-based advertising is popular with companies who want to raise brand awareness about their product or service; if you want to base your ad spending on sales or desired actions, focus on Click Through Rate (CTR) or Cost Per Action (CPA) advertising.

Reference Link:

http://adsense.blogspot.com/2006/02/ecpm-what-exactly-is-that.html

38. Awareness Advertising Ratio (AAR)

Equation: AAR= ACA/CAS X 100

Where CAS = Customer Awareness Spending, and

TAB = Total Advertising Budget.

Description: The Awareness Advertising Ratio determines the proportion of total advertising intended to raise brand awareness rather than to produce a direct response. (For example, giving away t-shirts displaying your company logo is brand awareness advertising –

unless the t-shirt says "Call Today for $5 Off All Purchases!").

Example: You spend $50,000 total on all your advertising efforts. $4,000 of that amount goes to activities like running brand awareness ads and contacting influential bloggers in hopes they will talk about your products, or sending free product samples to reviewers and influence leaders.

4,000/50,000 = .08, or 8%. 8% of your total advertising budget went to raising brand awareness.

Brand awareness is the degree to which potential customers recognize or recall your company name, product name, logo, products and services, etc. It does not mean customers will buy your products – having brand awareness does mean they know your product exists, and hopefully that they have some sense of the benefits of your product. The higher your brand awareness, the more people know about you; low brand awareness means you've barely created a ripple in the consumer consciousness pond.

Keep in mind brand awareness can be narrowly defined: If you sell a sophisticated software product used by the aerospace industry, you don't care if the average person knows about your product – the people you care about are the decision makers in the aerospace field.

Unless you sell a widely-used consumer product, spending money on brand awareness is typically less effective than spending on a more direct-response form of advertising. At the same time, some online businesses use social media as a form of brand awareness marketing; for example, say you sell golf clubs and you create a funny video showing golf clubs used to perform typical household tasks. If the video becomes an online hit, millions of people may become aware of your brand by watching the video – your advertising cost (in this case) is limited to the cost of producing the video.

The average online business should spend a small portion of its advertising budget on brand awareness, unless you find creative ways to make your brand awareness advertising go viral. Otherwise, focus on direct-response advertising where you can evaluate the effectiveness of your efforts – and make quick changes to improve your result.

Reference Link:

http://www.marketresearch.com/product/display.asp?prod uctid=1263406&xs=r&g=1&curr=USD&kw=&view=toc

39. Return on Marketing Investment (ROMI)

Equation: ROMI = RE/MI

Where RE = Revenues Earned, and

MI = Marketing Investment.

Description: Return on Marketing Investment determines the return on all forms of marketing expense. In theory, determining the ROMI indicates the expected change in total revenue if the advertising budget is increased or decreased.

Example: Last month you had total revenue of $37,000. You spent $2,350 total on all forms of advertising.

$37,000/$2,350 = $15.74. Your ROMI was $15.74 per thousand dollars spent on advertising.

The problem with ROMI is that it does not help you understand which of your marketing efforts work well and which do not. On the other hand, ROMI lets you understand the effectiveness of all your marketing efforts, especially if you include other costs of marketing. Take the example above; you spent $2,350 on advertising. But possibly you hired an advertising assistant to implement your strategies, and you paid that person $2,000. You could choose to lump salary cost in with your other marketing investment dollars – now you've spent $4,350 on advertising, and your ROMI decreases to $8.50 per dollar spent.

You're happy with the assistant's efforts, and you decide hiring another marketing assistant to spearhead increasing your presence on social media sites. You spend another $2,000 on salaries, and your revenues increase to $62,500. Your ROMI is now $9.8 per dollar spent – nice move!

Again, ROMI is directionally accurate. It is possible that sales increased because of another factor. Possibly an influential blogger raved about your product, and buyers flocked to your site. Use ROMI to provide an overall sense of the success of your marketing efforts; if you want to know how a particular form of advertising is working, you'll need to dig a little deeper.

Reference Link:
http://en.wikipedia.org/wiki/Return_on_marketing_invest ment

40. Average Order Size (AOS)

Equation: AOS = TSR/TNS

Where TSR = Total Sales Revenue, and

TNS = Total Number of Sales.

Description: Different customers order different amounts of products or services; Average Order Size determines the average sale, in terms of dollars, per each individual transaction. (Keep in mind the same customer could initiate multiple transactions; AOS determines sales per order, not sales per customer.)

Example: You sell t-shirts. Last month your sales totaled $32,500. You received 985 individual orders.

$32,500/985 = $32.99. Your AOS was $32.99.

AOS helps you understand the relationship of transaction costs to transactions. And, if you sell products with different price points, AOS can help you understand whether customers tend to order more expensive or less expensive products.

Say you determine that it costs you $1.50 to process each transaction. Your AOS is $10, and you make a profit (after expenses, including transaction costs, of $1. You would love to increase your profits, so you decide to reduce the price on certain items.)

Wait – raise profits by reducing prices? Does that make sense? In this case it does:

Cutting prices slightly on certain products could cause purchasers to add those products to their order. If that happens, you make more money on that sale because your transaction costs are spread over a larger AOS. In this case cutting a price by 10% could result in additional sales per order and actually increase your total profits. While your gross profit margin (GPM) on that item may fall, total profits may increase. (Remember, profit equals sales minus costs; what's important is not what you sell a product for, it's what portion of that sale you get to keep.)

Reference Link:
http://www.websiteceo.com/screenshots/hitlens/09.htm

41. Sales Growth (SG)

Equation: SG = CS/PS – 1

Where CS = Current Sales, and

PS = Previous Sales.

Description: Sales Growth evaluates current sales against sales from a previous period; for example, you could compare this month's sales to last month's sales, or this November's sales to last November's sales, or sales on a year-to-year basis. The result shows whether your sales are trending up or down, and at what rate.

Example: Last month you had sales of $12,578. This month your sales totaled $14,116.

14,116/12,578 = 1.12; 1.12 – 1 = .12, or 12%. Your total sales rose by 12%.

Tracking sales is important, but only in an overall sense in terms of the health of your business. If sales are up and profits are down, for example, have you really had a good month?

In any case, growth in sales is an indication that your marketing efforts are paying off and there is an increasing appetite for your products and services.

Reference Link: http://kpilibrary.com/?s=marketing

42. New Business Ratio (NBR)

Equation: NBR = NS/TS X 100

Where NS = New Sales, and

TS = Total Sales.

Description: The New Business Ratio helps you determine what portion of your sales can be attributed to current customers, and what portion can be attributed to acquiring new customers. The result helps you understand the effectiveness of your marketing efforts.

Example: Last month your sales totaled $20,000. Existing customers purchased $11,000 worth of services; new customers accounted for remainder.

11,000/20,000 = .55, or 55%. New business accounted for 55% of your total sales for the month.

Some industries rely on new business almost exclusively; for example, if you sell a product that can only be used once (for example, you're a wedding photographer), then your new business should make up almost all of your sales (unless one of your previous clients divorces and re-marries.)

The average business makes sales to previous customers. If you sell two e-books, a customer may purchase one e-book this month and another e-book next month; in that case he is a repeat customer, not a new customer.

If your NBR increases, that could mean two things: Your marketing efforts could be bringing in more qualified buyers, or your existing customers could be buying your products at a lower rate. (NBR rises and falls dependent on both of those factors, not on one factor in isolation.)

The key is to hang on to as many existing customers as possible while bringing in as much new business as possible. The NBR can help you determine how well you're holding on to your customers, and the relative success of your efforts to bring in new customers.

Reference Link: http://www.ad-mkt-review.com/public_html/docs/fs059.html

43. Customer Lifetime Value (CLV)

Equation: CLV = PV/C of the future cash flows expected from the customer relationship.

Where PV = Present Value of each customer, and

C = Customers.

Description: Customer Lifetime Value is the average value of customers over the term they are expected to do business with your company.

Example: Your average customer purchases products from you for two years. For the last two years your total sales are $300,000. You have 1,800 customers.

$300,000/1800 = $1,666. Your CLV is $1,666; each customer is "worth" $1,666 in sales.

Advertising is designed to bring in new customers (unless you're advertising to a mailing list made up of previous customers, for example). Once you have a customer, do your best not to let them go. CLV can help you determine just how valuable your customers are.

You may not have enough data to use to determine how long customers stay with you, and how much they spend over that "lifetime." That's okay; estimates are fine for now. But take the time to create tools to help you better understand long-term customer behavior; then you'll have a much better sense of how much you can afford to spend to acquire new customers.

If you want to increase CLV, focus on marketing to current customers: Stay in touch, create loyalty programs or special offers, make it easy for current customers to purchase additional products or services, and take steps to improve overall customer satisfaction. After all, it tends to cost a lot more to get a new customer than to retain a current customer.

Reference Link:
http://en.wikipedia.org/wiki/Customer_lifetime_value

44. Successful Strategies Index (SSI)

Equation: SSI = SE/TS X 100

Where SE = Strategies that meet Expectation, and

TS = Total Strategies adopted.

Description: Your company likely uses a variety of strategies to promote your products and services. The Successful Strategies Index determines the portion of those approaches that meet your goals.

Example: To market your service, you run ad campaigns, banner ads, use social media marketing like Digg, Facebook, Twitter, etc, and you use the services of a public relations firm to line up interviews by bloggers and other influential online presences. In total you undertake 15 separate marketing strategies. You have created goals for each strategy (in terms of sales, increase in site visitors, etc.) and determine that 9 of your strategies have met your expectations.

9/15= .6, or 60%. Your SSI is 60%.

Now – what does that tell you? Admittedly, not a lot about the specific results of each individual strategy, and the reasons why those strategies did or did not meet your expectations. But it does give you a feel for the overall success of your various strategies. SSI data can be especially important if you hire an outside firm to coordinate marketing or if you have persons inside your firm responsible for marketing. Their job should be to constantly increase SSI – and to set higher and higher expectations for success.

Reference Link: http://marketing.about.com/

45. Email Marketing Ratio (EMR)

Equation: EMR= EM/TS X 100

Where EM = Email Marketing revenue (revenues resulting from email marketing), and

TS = Total Sales.

Description: Email Marketing Revenue determines the portion of total sales derived from email marketing. (The basic formula can also be used to determine the portion of sales derived from other marketing tools.)

Example: Last month you had total of $68,400 in sales. You ran an email campaign that brought in $18,300.

18,300/68,400 = .26, or 26%. Email marketing was responsible for 26% of your total sales.

EMR can be used to evaluate any type of advertising expense. Using the example above, say you spent $4,300 on banner ads. As a result the BAMR (Banner Ad Marketing Rate) was 6.2%; 6.2% of your revenues came from banner advertising.

The key to a metric like EMR is that it helps you understand the relative contribution to total sales of your various marketing efforts. What it doesn't show is the efficiency of a particular effort; use (Return on Investment) ROI to determine how hard your advertising dollars are working for you.

Reference Link: http://www.spectruminc.com/internet-marketing-strategy/brand-development.aspx

46. Return on Investment (ROI)

Equation: ROI = (R – CI /) CI X 100

Where R = Return, and

CI = Cost of Investment.

Definition: Return on Investment is a performance metric used to determine the efficiency of a particular investment; higher ROI indicates an investment producing a solid return.

Example: You decide to run an email marketing campaign. The cost of the campaign is $1,500. As a result of the campaign you generated $8,300 in new sales.

8,300 – 1,500 = 6,800; 6,800/1,500 = 4.53, or 453%. Your ROI was 453%.

ROI should be used to determine the specific results from a specific campaign or expense. It's not only useful for determining advertising efficiency; it can be used as a quick way to determine the value of any kind of spending or investment. It's a simple tool, but it helps provide a quantifiable answer to a very basic management question:

"Should I do this?"

Reference Link:
http://www.investopedia.com/terms/r/returnoninvestment.asp

47. Anonymous Visitor Conversion Rate (AVCR)

Equation: AVCR = NVC / TC X 100

Where NVC = Anonymous Visitors Converted, and

TC = Total Conversions.

Description: The AVCR determines which portion of conversions can be attributed to new visitors, and which portion comes from existing customers or subscribers.

Example: You manage an information-based website, and allow subscribers to access a variety of resources. You create a new white paper visitors can download for free, without subscribing. Last month 10,000 people downloaded the white paper. 17,500 downloads came from current site subscribers; 2,500 can be attributed to new subscribers or anonymous visitors.

2,500/20,000 = .125, or 12.5%. Your AVCR was 12.5% for the new white paper.

AVCR helps determine whether particular offers succeed in generating action from new site visitors. (Converting existing customers is good, but converting new visitors is great.) Evaluating AVCR can help you determine if a particular product or offer helps to attract additional business.

Here's another example. Say you sell a variety of products. You add a new product to your line. Your AVCR for that product is 90%; it's popular with new visitors, and has brought new customers to your site, but your existing customers show little interest. Is that a problem?

Maybe – or maybe not. You may have added the product to your line with the express intent of bringing in new customers. If that's the case, you've succeeded.

On the other hand, if you hoped existing customers would leap at the chance to purchase the new product, it looks as if you've failed. In either case, AVCR helped you understand the relationship between the buying habits of existing customers and the buying habits of new customers.

Again, keep in mind conversions don't have to be sales. A conversion is simply a desired action; if you hope new visitors will be enticed to take that action, a high AVCR is just what you're looking for.

Reference: N/A

48. Leads Generated Index (LGI)

Equation: LGI = (NLG − PLG) / PLG X 100

Where NLG = New Leads Generated, and

PLG = Previous Leads Generated

Description: The Leads Generated Index determines the increase or decrease in leads generated on a percentage basis. LGI shows whether a website has succeeded over a specified time period in attracting new leads, and at what rate.

Example: Last year your website generated 500 leads. This year you generated 568 leads.

568 − 500 = 68; 68/500 = .136, or 13.6%. Your LGI increased by 13.6%.

There are at least two different ways to employ the LGI. One is to determine whether your website succeeds in producing leads. The other is to determine the effectiveness of advertising or lead-generation efforts. If you're an affiliate marketer and you pay by the lead, your LGI isn't particularly critical; you want your LGI to rise, but if it doesn't, at least you're not paying a flat rate for advertising. If you pay an employee (or a firm) a fixed fee to help generate leads, or if you run Cost per Thousand (CMP) or flat-rate advertising intended to generate new leads, then you definitely want your LGI to increase to justify the expense.

Reference Link: N/A

Category: Servers and Technology

49. Percentage Uptime (PU)

Equation: PU= U/T X 100

Where U = Uninterrupted service time, and

T = total Time.

Definition: Percentage Uptime calculates the percentage of time that service was available, with no downtime or problems with features or applications.

Example: During a 30-day month, total time equals 720 hours or 43,200 minutes. Total downtime equals 14 minutes.

43,200 − 14 = 43,186; 43,186/43,200 = .99967, or 99.967%. Uptime is 99.967%

Percentage uptime is a key metric for web hosting; after all, if your site is down, customers can't access you. Recent advances in cloud computing and server redundancy has allowed some web hosting companies to claim 99.999% uptime; if that is indeed the case, service will only be unavailable for a little over five minutes per year.

The more visitors you have − or expect to have − the more critical PU becomes. If you only average twenty or thirty visitors a day, uptime isn't as critical; if you average thousands of visitors a day, a ten-minute service outage could result in a number of lost customers.

Reference Link: http://blog.clickfire.com/realmetrics-web-hosting-metrics/

50. Average Time to Provision (ATP)

Equation: ATP = TT/NP

Where TT = Total Time, and

NP = Number of Provisions.

Definition: A provision is an event; for example, a provision could be adding a new function to a pre-existing service. (You could think of a provision as an event completion of a task.) The Average Time to Provision is an average of the time it takes to add new functions or services.

Example: Your programming consultant adds 18 new customer functions to your database package. In total, he spends 3.5 hours developing and implementing these functions.

3.5 X 60 = 210 minutes; 210/18 = 11.66. The ATP for installing these functions is 11.66 minutes per function.

AVP can also be used to determine the average time of a variety of functions. For example, you run a massive shopping site; you have thousands of products available. You add new product descriptions, photos, etc., to an offline database, and then periodically upload the data to your website. An application adds the data to the proper sections of the website, updates links, etc. ATP can be used to measure the average time it takes for the new data to become available to users; if you upload 30 new products and it takes four minutes for the application to complete the process, the ATP is .13 minutes, or 7.8 seconds.

Or, ATP could be used to measure the effectiveness of other functions. Say a customer can enter data about, for example, a type of loan they are interested in; you could have an application that searches for potential lenders and returns that result. The ATP would be the average time the process takes to complete and display data to the customer.

A good example is what happens when you use a travel site to search for available flights; the time it takes for all requests to be completed, divided by the total number of requests, is the ATP for the flight search function.

Reference Link:
http://www.knowledgetransfer.net/dictionary/ITIL/en/Mean_Time_to_Provision.htm

51. Minimum Bandwidth Guarantee (MBG)

Equation: MBG = the Minimum Bandwidth Guaranteed to be available at any time

Description: This metric does not require a calculation; the provider determines the value. If a provider guarantees at least 15MBps, then at no time should available bandwidth be less than 15MBps.

Example: Your Internet Service Provider (ISP) guarantees 12MBps of bandwidth will always be available. Higher bandwidth may often be available; 12MBps is the minimum expectation. You have determined that your functions require a minimum of 10MBps before bandwidth will cause problems or create unwanted delays. As long as the provider meets this MBG, functions will meet your expectations.

An ISP tries to balance demand with supply. Installing the infrastructure to handle occasional spikes in demand would cause capacity to be idle much of the time. By setting a MBG, the ISP sets a "floor" for bandwidth in the knowledge that much of the time the bandwidth available will be much higher.

Your goal is to ensure the MGB meets your needs. If you need to transfer massive amounts of data in a short period of time, high bandwidth is critical. (Keep in mind you may pay more for this privilege.) If not, a lower MGB may suit your needs and ease the strain on your ISP costs.

Reference Link:
http://www.eecs.wsu.edu/~dawn/Slides/MBG-OWns.ppt

52. Failed Transaction Rate (PFR)

Equation: FTR = (FT/TT) X 100

Where FT = Failed Transactions, and

TT = Total Transactions.

Description: Failed Transaction Rate determines the rate of failed transactions compared to all transactions executed during a specified period of time. FTR is especially important for websites and applications that perform a large number of transactions. FTR is not designed to measure transactions abandoned by a user, like shopping cart abandonment; it is designed to measure system or application errors.

Example: You run an online shopping site with thousands of products in your database. Visitors can search for products using a variety of keywords. Over the course of a month, visitors perform searches 20,000 times. Of those searches, 138 fail due to system errors.

138/20,000 = .0069, or .69%. Your FTR is .69%. (Of course, that also means that 138 potential customers could have been lost because they did not find what they were looking for.)

Nothing is perfect, even though we would like it to be – even software. If you hire a developer to create an application, or you purchase a sophisticated application, a key specification might be the Failed Transaction Rate. (Obviously the rate should be as small as possible.)

Another use of FTR is to determine when additional development spending makes sense. Say you have a search function on your site; it does a decent job, but 3% of the time it fails to deliver a result, even when appropriate results were available. You may decide that you can live with a 3% failure rate; if not, spend money to improve your search function and track the results to ensure the overall FTR improves.

Reference Link:
http://www.certagon.com/WhitePapers/TransactionComp letion-TheNewPerformanceMetric.pdf

53. Transactions Executed within Response Time (TERT)

Equation: TERT = TES/TT X 100

Where TES = Transactions Exceeding Standard, and

TT = Total Transactions.

Description: The Transaction Executed within Response Time metric determines the percentage of transactions that were completed within pre-determined time limits.

Example: You determine that online payment transactions should take no more than 45 seconds to complete. You process 3,400 total transactions; 92 of those transactions take longer than 45 seconds to complete.

92/3,400 = .027, or 2.7%. Your TERT is 2.7%.

TERT can be used to evaluate a variety of processes, not just application transactions. For example, say you determine that all orders will be shipped within twenty-four hours; you can measure your performance against this standard using TERT. Or you might set a standard response time to an e-mail query; you can measure your performance to this standard using TERT.

In computer technology terms, TERT is frequently used to set a standard for – and measure performance against – applications under development. If you hire a developer to create a new application, set a TERT rate the developer must meet; if the rate exceeds your standard, the application has not been developed to your satisfaction.

Reference Link: www.ittoolbox.com

54. Backup Encryption Percentage (BEP)

Equation: BEP = (ED/TD) X 100

Where ED = Encrypted Data, and

TD =Total Data.

Description: Backup Encryption Percentage measures the ratio of backed-up data that is encrypted against the total data encrypted. BEP is a critical factor where data security is important.

Example: You back up 100GB of data each week. 60GB is encrypted.

$60/100 = .6$, or 60%. Your BEP is 60%.

Is 60% sufficient? It depends on the nature of your data. If all the data you back up is sensitive (customer information, phone numbers, credit card numbers, payment histories, etc), then a 60% BEP means 40% of your data is insecure and open to attack. If that data becomes exposed due to theft or loss, not only can your reputation be damaged, but you may be subject to fines or penalties as well.

Reference Link:
http://www.symantec.com/business/resources/articles/article.jsp?aid=encrypting_critical_backup_data

55. Average Offsite Backup Restore Time (AOBRT)

Equation: AOTRB = TRT/TNT

Where TRT = Total Restore Time, and

TNT = Total Number of Restores.

Description: This metric evaluates the average amount of time required to restore data that has been backed up offsite.

Example: Your data is backed up offsite by a commercial backup firm. The amount of data backed up is relatively stable. To test the service, you perform a series of backup restores and time the result: You perform 10 backups, for a total elapsed time of 138 hours.

138/10 = 13.8. The average time it takes to restore data backed up offsite is 13.8 hours.

Onsite data backup restoration tends to be slower (of course, depending on bandwidth). In general, though, tape or hard drive backups tend to be quicker. At the same time, onsite backups are less safe, especially in the case of fire or natural disaster. Determining the Average Offsite Backup Restore Time – using your data and your systems so you can evaluate your results, and not an "average" result – will help you determine if the speed of an offsite backup is sufficient to support critical operations.

Reference Link: http://kpilibrary.com/categories/backup

56. Average Age of Backups (AAB)

Equation: AAB = B/T

Where B = Backups, and

T = Time.

Description: The Average Age of Backups measures the average elapsed time between data backups. The longer the AAB, the more data could possibly be lost in the event of a failure.

Example: You want your accounting data to be backed up often. You direct your IT staff to create a system so one backup per hour, on a 24-hour basis, is performed. You check results from the previous day and find that 21 backups were performed.

24/21 = 1.14. The AAB of your backups is 1.14 hours, which is "older" than the 1 hour "age" you required.

AAB is not only an internal metric; it can also be used to evaluate the performance of a vendor. A long AAB indicates a company does not have sufficient systems in place – or sufficient motivation – to ensure that critical data is backed up in a timely manner. If another party will hold data on your behalf, make sure the AAB meets your needs and standards.

Reference Link: http://kpilibrary.com/categories/backup

57. Average Backup Restore Time (ABRT)

Equation: ABRT = TRT/TNT

Where TRT = Total Restore Time, and

TNT = Total Number of Restores.

Description: This metric evaluates the average amount of time required to restore data that has been backed up onsite.

Example: Your data is backed up onsite either by tape or hard drive. To test how quickly you can restore data in the event of a failure, you perform a series of backup restores and time the result: You perform 5 backups for a total elapsed time of 22 hours.

22/5 = 4.4. It takes 4.4 hours to restore data backed up onsite.

ABRT is similar to Average Offsite Backup Restore Time (AOBRT); the only difference is that in this case your data is backed up onsite. The speed of a backup is based on the amount of data, the type of storage devices used, and the skill of your IT team. If your ABRT is too slow and will result in lost business or customer complaints, take steps to increase the speed at which backups can be performed.

Reference Link:
http://publib.boulder.ibm.com/infocenter/idshelp/v10/ind
ex.jsp?topic=/com.ibm.bar.doc/barmst46.htm

58. Percentage of Dead Servers (PDS)

Equation: PDS = (SNU/TSA) X 100

Where SNU = Servers Not Used, and

TSA = Total Servers Available.

Description: Percentage of Dead Servers does not refer only to servers that are unavailable due to some type of failure; a "dead" server can also be a server that has little to no CPU utilization due to a lack of demand.

Example: You maintain 75 servers in your data warehouse. Due to a lack of demand, 12 servers are used less than 1% of the time and are considered "dead."

12/75 = .16, or 16%. 16% of your servers are for all practical purposes not used.

Which means, of course, that you probably have too many servers: Move the data to other servers and shut them down (or sell them.)

PDS can also be used to evaluate expenses if you pay an outside firm for server use. Say you determined you would need 20 servers to handle your data and your processes. If you are charged for the use of 20 servers but for all practical purposes 4 of those servers are dead, reduce the number of servers you pay for. (The provider should be able to generate timely reports showing server usage for any specified time period.)

Reference Link:
http://kpilibrary.com/categories/systems

59. Average Time to Repair (ATR)

Equation: ATR = TTR/TR

Where TTR = Total Time of Repairs, and

TR = Total Repairs.

Definition: Average Time to Repair determines the average elapsed time between when an incident is reported and corrective repairs are completed.

Example: You run a help center with 300 employees providing online help to customers. Computers fail on a regular basis for a variety of reasons, and your technical team is called upon to make repairs and get the workstation up and running. Over the course of a month 26 failures are reported; total time to make repairs is 62 hours.

62/26 = 2.38. Your Average Time to Repair is 2.38 hours.

ATR is often built into maintenance or service contracts. Say you hire an outside firm to deal with computer problems. If you need an ART of 2 hours, for example, the cost of the contract may be relatively high, since the outside firm will need to be sufficiently staffed and prepared to make repairs within that time period. If you specify an ART of 24 hours, the cost will likely be lower – and if you agree to an ART of 5 days, the cost should be lower still.

Average Time to Repair can determine the speed of other events. For example, you could track the Average Time to Respond. In that case, you would measure how quickly a technician responds to a query or arrives at your location.

Or, if you have redundant capability that automatically kicks in when equipment fails, you could measure Average Time to Return to Service, which is the time it takes a technician to restore the equipment to proper function. Even though your systems stayed running, you lost redundant capacity for the time it took to return that equipment to proper function, so how quickly that redundancy is restored is important to you.

Reference Link:
http://en.wikipedia.org/wiki/Mean_time_to_repair

Category: Web Design Perspective

60. Navigability Rating

Equation: Navigability Rating measured on a scale of 1 to 10

Description: Ease of navigation is critical for web success. The Navigability Rating attempts to determine the ease of use and simplicity of the navigation structure by measuring the design against a pre-determined set of criteria.

Example: You wish to determine how easy your website is to navigate. You establish a set of criteria that you feel are important to your customers: How easy it is to find the search tool, how quickly the user can determine which category to choose to find a desired product, the ease of the shopping cart checkout process, etc. User feedback is gathered and an overall NR is computed based on all the data acquired.

Keep in mind a NR is subjective. Some researchers have developed statistical packages that measure NR based on usage data, server log files, and structural complexity. While you could choose to engage a consultant to perform an in-depth NR assessment, start by asking your customers what they think. They'll tell you, especially if you give them an incentive for participating in your survey. Plus, their opinion is the most important opinion – their use of your website pays your bills.

Reference Link:
http://eserver.org/courses/w01/tc510/edgar/Denise/denise9.htm

61. Average Designer Pages Released (ADPR)

Equation: ADPR = TPR/TD

Where TPR = Total Pages Released, and

TD = Total Designers.

Description: Average Designer Pages Released indicates the efficiency of a design team (and can help indicate the relative efficiency of each member). ADPR can also be measured against industry standards to determine efficiency.

Example: Your in-house design team releases 26 new pages a day. The team is made up of 8 full-time designers.

26/8 = 3.25. Your ADPR is 3.25 pages per day.

Keep in mind you'll need to compare apples to apples. If your team works on complex pages, expect the overall rate to decrease; if pages are relatively simple, the rate should increase.

You can also use ADPR to evaluate individual designers. If your ADPR is 3.25 and one designer averages releasing 5 pages per day, she is clearly more effective than the "average" designer. (Assuming the quality of the pages meets standards, of course.) A designer averaging 2 pages released per day is performing well below average.

ADPR can also be used to measure the performance of an external design team. If you pay based on an hourly rate, hiring a team capable of generating a high ADPR will cut your costs. If you pay by the project, the ADPR is less of a concern – unless the ADPR is too slow to meet your project needs.

Reference Link:
http://eserver.org/courses/w01/tc510/edgar/Denise/denise9.htm

62. Project on Time Ratio (POT)

Equation: POT = PCT/TP X 100

Where PCT = Projects Completed on Time, and

TP = Total Projects.

Description: This ratio determines the percentage of projects completed on time, measuring the performance of your organization or of specific in-house or external teams against pre-determined goals.

Example: You initiate 37 projects. 34 of those projects are completed on time.

34/37 = .918, or 91.8%. Over 90% of your projects were completed on time.

Project On Time Ratio measures performance and can also help you predict future events. For example, if your team averages a POT of 95% on a specific type of project, you can safely predict that 95 of the 100 projects they undertake next month will be completed on time. Or you can use the metric to track month-to-month performance, and determine whether process improvement efforts are having a positive effect.

POT is also used to evaluate outside contractors. Say you ask an outside firm to complete 450 discreet tasks; you could specify in the contract that 80% of all projects must be completed on time. You may even build penalties into the contract in case that standard is not met.

Reference Link: N/A

63. Average Page Size (APS)

Equation: APS = TFS/TP

Where TFS = Total File Size, and

TP = No. of Pages.

Description: Average Page Size determines the average file size of an individual web page. Pages with large file sizes take longer to load and require more bandwidth. APS is intended to monitor page size "creep" as additional functions and objects are added to pages throughout the size.

Example: The total file size of all pages on your site is 49,000k. Your site is made up of 239 individual pages.

49,000/239 = 205. Your Average Page Size is 205k.

Page file sizes have grown dramatically in the last few years as users continue to add images, video, objects, applications, and other functions to their websites. Between 2003 and 2008 the APS has nearly tripled. While offering additional functions and capabilities can help attract and keep more visitors, increasing page file sizes can slow page load times and increase file storage and bandwidth needs.

APS lets you determine the growth in file size of your average web page. As more users convert to higher-bandwidth connections, the APS is potentially less important, at least to the user... but you should make every effort to keep file sizes low so that pages load quickly and the user experience is positive.

Reference Link:
http://www.websiteoptimization.com/speed/tweak/averag
e-web-page/

64. Pages Per Hour (PPH)

Equation: HPP = TP/TWH

Where TP = Total Pages developed, and

TWH = Total Work Hours.

Description: Pages Per Hour measures the efficiency of a design team or an individual designer.

Example: You have six designers on staff. This week they worked 320 total hours and designed 210 pages.

320/210 = 1.476. Your team designed 1.476 pages per hour.

Pages Per Hour is strictly a productivity measurement. It can be used to measure any repeatable process: Shipping packages, processing orders, entering invoices, or in this case, pages designed per hour.

Keep in mind that complex pages should take longer to complete than simple pages. Designing a new page should take longer than making small modifications to an existing design. Always compare apples to apples as best possible. And be sure to take into account minor fluctuations in short-term activity; PPH is best measured over a relatively long time period, like days or weeks. The more data you have available, the more accurately you can determine PPH.

Reference Link:
http://eserver.org/courses/w01/tc510/edgar/Denise/denise9.htm

65. Projects Under Budget Ratio (PUBR)

Equation: PUBR = (PCWB/TP) X 100

Where PCWB = Projects Completed Within Budget

TP = Total Projects.

Description: This metric measures the percentage of projects that were completed at or under budget against the total number of projects completed successfully; the result evaluates the success rate of a team in meeting budget restrictions.

Example: You establish a set budget for every project your company undertakes. Teams take on a number of projects each month; last month your organization completed 83 projects. 75 of those projects were completed on- or under-budget.

75/83 = .903, or 90.3%. Your PUBR for the month was 90.3%.

The Projects Under Budget Ratio provides an indication of the overall success rate of your teams. If a project goes over budget it could be due to a number of factors: The initial budget was unrealistically low, the team was inefficient and spent more than should have been required, unexpected problems arose that increased costs, etc. Your goal is to complete 100% of your projects under budget – without setting a budget that is easy to meet, of course.

Tracking PUBR over time helps you evaluate the accuracy of your budgeting project and the efficiency and effectiveness of your teams. This metric can also be used to evaluate external suppliers; if you are charged based on time and materials and not a fixed project cost, PUBR can help you identify suppliers who "estimate low" and "complete high."

Reference Link:
http://www.demandmetric.com/content/practical-tools/website-design-budget

Category: Accounting

66. Current Ratio (CR)

Equation: CR = CA/CL

Where CA = Current Assets, and

CL = Current Liabilities.

Description: The Current Ratio (sometimes called the Working Capital Ratio) measures a company's liquidity. A high CR indicates the company has sufficient cash or assets to meet normal operating conditions. A low CR could mean the company uses more of its assets to grow the business. Assets are cash and other items that could be converted to cash; liabilities are debts and obligations that are expected to be settled within a year.

Example: Your business has total assets of $500,000. Your current liabilities (the money you owe) total $120,000.

500,000 / 100,000 = 4.16. Your Current Ratio is 4.16. (Keep in mind that if assets equal liabilities, your Current Ratio is 1.)

In most industries, if your CR is over 2 your company is generally considered to have good short-term financial strength. If your CR is under 1, and your liabilities exceed your assets, you're clearly struggling, at least in the short term. (Hopefully major revenues are around the corner.)

Another way to view CR is in dollar terms. Say you have assets of $100 and liabilities totaling $34. (Obviously we're keeping the math simple.) Your CR is 2.94, or, put another way, you have $2.94 in assets for every dollar you owe.

Comparing your CR over time is helpful. If your CR decreases, that could be an indication you are carrying too much inventory or you are struggling to collect receivables in a timely fashion. If you're not taking on more debt and your revenues are increasing, then your CR should improve – or something is wrong.

Reference link:
http://www.netmba.com/finance/financial/ratios/

67. Net Working Capital Ratio (NWCR)

Equation: NWC = NWC - TA

Where NWC = Net Working Capital, and

   TA = Total Assets.

Description: Working capital is the money used to run a business and pay liabilities. Net Working Capital measures cash flow to determine if a business has sufficient funds to maintain normal operations.

Example: Your total assets are $1,00,000. That includes your building, vehicles, cash, inventory – everything. Your working capital totals $600,000, including cash and other liquid assets.

600,000 / 1,000,000 = .6, or 60%. Your Net Working Capital Ratio is 60%.

If you're confused about the difference between assets and working capital, look at it this way: Cash is an asset – you can use it for a variety of purposes, including paying employee salaries. Your building is also an asset, but unless you're willing to sell the building (which may put you out of business), it's not working capital – it's just an asset. The expensive painting in your lobby is an asset, but it's not working capital; you can't pay your lease with it. So, the NWCR evaluates how much of your assets are liquid and how many are relatively non-liquid – which is an indication of the health of your operation.

In short, think of working capital as the money you use to run the business. The more of your assets that are working capital, the more liquid your company is and the better it can respond to changing business conditions.

Also keep in mind lenders often look at your NWCR over time to determine whether you could weather short and longer-term dips in sales and revenue. Many lenders require you to meet a minimum NWCR to qualify for loans.

Improving your NWCR is both easy and difficult; keep spending to a minimum, try hard not to tie up your funds in fixed assets, and keep inventories low – that way more of your money is available to run the business instead of fuel your interest in lobby art.

Reference Link: http://cpaclass.com/fsa/ratio-01a.htm

68. Return on Assets (ROA)

Equation: ROA = NI/TA

Where NI = Net Income, and

TA = Total Assets.

Description: Return on Assets measures how much profit a company made for every dollar in assets. How hard is your money working for you? ROA lets you know.

Example: You have net income of $100,000 this month. Your total assets equal $65,000.

$100,000 / $65,000 = $1.53. You earned $1.53 for every dollar in assets.

Shareholders are especially interested in ROA; it measures the return on the money they have invested in the company. But ROA can vary wildly based on your industry; if you manufacturer automobiles (and if you do, I feel sorry for you), a lot of your money is tied up in expensive equipment and large buildings. Your ROA will be relatively low as a result. (In general terms, a capital-intensive business should have a relatively low ROA.)

On the other hand, if you run a consulting business out of your house your ROA should be very high because you should need very few fixed assets to maintain operations.

ROA can also be used to compare companies in similar industries. Say one company has net income of $100,000 and total assets of $200,000; the ROA is .50 per $1 in assets, or an ROA of 50%. Say another company earns $100,000 but has assets of $125,000; the ROA is .80 per $1 in assets, or an ROA of 80%.

Which is doing a better job with its investment? Which company would you invest in? Which company would you consider purchasing? It's easy to tell.

Since ROA measures your return based on all the resources you had at your disposal, it's a very easy way to determine how effectively you're running your business – and if you want to attract investors, a high ROA is one way to do it.

Reference Link:
http://beginnersinvest.about.com/cs/investinglessons/l/blr eturnonasset.htm

69. Return on Equity (ROE)

Equation: ROE = NI/ SE X 100

Where NI = Net Income, and

SE = Stockholder Equity.

Description: Equity is what is left on a balance sheet after all liabilities are taken care of. If you've invested in a company, that equity is your money (even though you may have invested more than your equity is now worth.)

Return on Equity measures how well your money is being used, and what return you receive for your investment.

Example: Let's keep things really simple. Your neighbor is starting a business; you lend him $100 in return for an ownership stake. (He gives you 10% of the company because he now has $1,000 in capital to work with.) In his first month of operation, he makes a profit of $500. Since you own 10% of the company, your piece of the $500 is $50.

$50 / 100 = .50$, or 50%. You received a 50% ROE.

Return on Equity is similar to Return on Assets (ROA) because it provides an indication of how well a company is managing its assets. In simple terms, ROE shows you how a company is doing with the money it currently has, while ROA can indicate how well a company would do if additional capital is invested (and all other business conditions remained stable).

Keep in mind ROE may be meaningless in some circumstances. Say you run own a company and are the sole employee. When you started the company you invested $10,000 from your savings. You bring in revenue, pay expenses and liabilities (including a little of your original loan), and take the remaining funds as salary. Your "return on equity" comes in the form of salary – but since salaries count against company income, at the end of the year your company didn't "make money" even though you did.

Make sense? Public companies have ROE; many small companies do not, at least under traditional financial calculations.

ROE is a key measurement used by many investors, including Warren Buffet. Why? It's simple: If you plan to invest your money, you should expect a return on that investment – the higher the return the better.

While lenders don't place much emphasis on ROE, investors do.

Reference Link:
http://beginnersinvest.about.com/cs/investinglessons/l/blreturnequity.htm

70. Earnings per Share (EPS)

Equation: EPS = NI/ NOCS

Where NI = Net Income, and

NOCS = Number of Outstanding Common Shares.

Description: Earnings per share is a metric used to evaluate the income of a company to its total number of shares. EPS can be calculated for the previous year, which is a company's "trailing EPS," for the current year, "current EPS," or for the next year, which is "forward EPS." (Keep in mind forward EPS is only an estimate, because next year hasn't actually happened yet, and if it's early in this year, current EPS is basically an estimate, too.)

Example: Your firm has ten shares of stock outstanding. (You own them all, even though that doesn't matter for the purposes of this example.) Your earnings last year were $10,000.

$10,000 /1,000 = $10. Last year you had earnings per share of $10.

Earnings per share is a critical financial measurement, especially for publicly-traded companies. While raw earnings are important – because, after all, if your company made a million dollars last year, that's a good thing – investors care about earnings per share because it takes into account fluctuations in the number of shares outstanding.

For example, say last year Rocket Golf Clubs, Inc. had earnings of $1,000,000. There are 1,000,000 shares outstanding, so EPS are $1. This year earnings double to $2,000,000. Better year?

Maybe… but what if Rocket sold 2,000,000 new shares of stock at the beginning of the year to finance an expansion? Earnings doubled, but total shares outstanding more than doubled; as a result, this year's EPS fell to .66. For investors, that's not a great result after all.

The media tends to report financial results in terms of earnings per share. A statement like, "Earnings fell from $2.36 per share to $2.15 per share," is based on the EPS formula, and gives investors a way to quantify company results, eliminating changes in the total number of outstanding shares as a variable.

Reference Link: http://cpaclass.com/fsa/ratio-01a.htm

71. Assets Turnover Ratio (ATR)

Equation: ATR = TR/TA

Where TR = Total Revenue, and

TA = Total Assets.

Description: The Asset Turnover Ratio calculates the amount of sales generated from each dollar of assets. Companies with low profit margins tend, on average, to have high asset turnover, while companies with high profit margins tend to have low asset turnover. This ratio is useful to determine the amount of sales that are generated from each dollar of assets. As noted above, companies with low profit margins tend to have high asset turnover, those with high profit margins have low asset turnover.

Example: Rocket Golf Clubs, Inc. has total revenue of $125,000. Company assets total $100,000.

125,000 / 100,000 = 1.25. Assets "turned over" 1.25 times, or 125%; put differently, $1.25 in sales was generated from every $1 in assets.

The best way to evaluate ATV is to compare one company to others in the same industry. Automotive and heavy manufacturing companies tend to have low ATVs;

in many cases the ATV will be less than 1. A retailer may have an ATV of 10 or more; little equipment or capital expenses are required, and product (hopefully) moves at a brisk pace.

But keep in mind that if your ATV is higher than the industry average, it could be because you haven't invested in replacing or improving outdated equipment, buildings, etc. For now you're doing well – but eventually you may have to make capital investments that will lower your ATV. For a few years your ATV may be lower than industry average – but the investments you've made in equipment may pay off in years to come.

Reference Link: http://cpaclass.com/fsa/ratio-01a.htm

72. Debt to Equity Ratio (DER)

Equation: DER = TL/TSE

Where TL = Total Liabilities, and

TSE = Total Stockholder Equity

Description: Debt to Equity indicates the amount of money a company owes compared to what it owns; it indicates the proportion of debt and equity a company uses to finance its assets and operations. A high debt to equity ratio could indicate that the company has borrowed too heavily; a low debt to equity ratio typically indicates the company generates working capital through its operations rather than by borrowing. In general, a DER over 1 indicates assets are financed largely through debt, while a DER under 1 indicates shareholder equity is the main source of financing.

Example: Rocket Golf Clubs, Inc. has total liabilities of $50,000. Shareholder equity totals $200,000.

50,000 / 200,000 = .25. The DER is .25.

A low ratio of .25 means Rocket Golf Clubs uses, for the most part, equity to finance operations. As a result, the company has little exposure to rising interest rates or nervous bankers. (On the other hand, investors may be pushing for a greater return on their investment.) Rocket could choose to take on more debt or buy back some of the outstanding shares; either would result in an increase in DER.

Let's look at the flip side of this scenario. Say you calculate that Rocket Golf Clubs has a DER of 3; it's carrying a lot of debt relative to investor equity. That makes the company nervous; one way to reduce the DER would be to sell additional shares of stock and use the proceeds to pay down debt. The DER would decrease, but investors may not be happy because their ownership stake becomes more diluted every time additional shares of stock are issued.

The DER is closely monitored by both investors and lenders. Lenders are especially concerned, since a high DER can create liquidity problems that could lead to loan defaults. (If I don't have money to pay, and my debt cripples my operations.) Banks sometimes step in and require companies to use excess cash flow to pay down debt, restrict further investments, and even require investors to put more equity into the company so the DER is decreased.

So what is a good DER? It depends on the industry, but in general terms a DER of .3 or .4 is considered healthy.

A quick note: Sometimes you'll see the DER shown as a percentage; a 30% DER is the same as a .3 DER; a company with a 200% DER (a DER of 2) has twice as much debt as equity.

Reference Link:
http://www.netmba.com/finance/financial/ratios/

73. Inventory Turnover Ratio (ITR)

Equation: ITR = CGS/I

Where CGS = Cost of Goods Sold, and

I = Inventory average value.

Description: The Inventory Turnover ratio reflects how many times a company's inventory is sold (and replaced) over a specified period of time. Inventory can include materials and supplies, finished products, work in progress, or a combination of all types of inventory. The higher the ratio, the more quickly inventory is turned over.

Example: Last year your average inventory value of your finished goods (you took a physical inventory on the 1st of every month, and calculated the value of your inventory each time) was $10,000. You sold $15,000 worth of finished goods during the year.

15,000 / 10,000 = 1.5. Your ITR was 1.5; you "turned" your inventory 1.5 times.

Turning your inventory as frequently as possible is critical; the less you have invested in inventory, the more cash you free up for other purposes. (That's why just-in-time purchasing and inventory systems are so popular.) Say, for example, you have $10,000 in inventory, and you sell $10,000 worth of goods. Your ITR is 1. If you could cut your inventory value in half, to $5,000, and still sell $10,000 worth of goods, your ITR increases to 2 ... without losing any sales. The $5,000 can be used for other purposes: Paying off debt, expanding operations, increasing marketing efforts ... whatever you decide.

Here's an example. Say you sell golf balls, and you like to keep a lot of stock on hand "just in case" a huge order comes in. You like to have three months worth of inventory on hand at any time.

The problem is, those huge orders never come in and your warehouse stays relatively full for months at a time. The golf balls that fill up your warehouse represent dollars that are not working for you – they're just taking up space. If you find a supplier who can fill orders in a week or less, you could keep two to three weeks worth of inventory on hand (or less), and free up cash for other purposes.

Keep in mind that if you sell a variety of products, some of your stock will turn more quickly, while less popular items will turn more slowly. That's okay – simply increase inventory levels on popular items, and decrease inventory levels on slow-moving items. Feel free to compare your ITR to other firms in your industry, but in the end, your only competition is you. Working hard to reduce your average inventory value increases your ITR and ensures your money works harder for you.

Reference Link: http://cpaclass.com/fsa/ratio-01a.htm

74. Debt Service Coverage Ratio (DSCR)

Equation: DSCR= NOI/TDS

Where NOI = Net Operating Income, and

TDS = Total Debt Service.

Description: Debt Coverage Service Ratio can have a variety of applications, but those applications all evaluate the same basic factors. Simply put, your ratio of funds generated by operating income to funds needed to service debt obligations lets you know if your cash flow is sufficient to cover your liabilities.

Examples: Your company has a variety of loans on the books: You've borrowed to purchase equipment, purchase inventory, and buy your own warehouse. Each month you make principal and interest payments on those loans totaling $10,000. Each month your net income is $12,000.

12,000 / 10,000 = 1.2. In short, you generate enough income to service your debt (with some money left over.)

Obviously if you're running a healthy business your DSCR should be over 1.0. (Hopefully your DSCR is significantly higher than 1.0.)

If your DSCR is, for example, .75, that means each month you only bring in 75% of the funds needed to make the necessary payments on your obligations. Your cash flow is negative and drastic measures are needed. If you're planning to start a business and you estimate you'll have negative cash flow, the difference will have to be made up from savings or from other income – at least until your DCSR reaches 1.0. (But keep in mind a DSCR of 1.0 means you're not making any money – you're just treading water.)

If you're trying to get a loan, a high DSCR makes a lender more comfortable because solid positive cash flow means funds are available to repay the loan. You may want as large a loan as possible, though, which means your resulting DSCR will be fairly low. (If your income stays the same and your debt increases, your DSCR automatically decreases. If income increases and debt stays the same, your DSCR automatically increases.) On average, most lenders look for a DSCR of at least 1.25; some require DSCRs of 1.5 or greater.

Even if you don't want a loan, a high DSCR means you're cash-flow positive and doing well.

Reference Link:
http://www.investopedia.com/terms/d/dscr.asp

75. Economic Value Added (EVA)

Equation: EVA = NOPAT – CC

Where NOPAT = Net Operating Profits After Taxes, and

CC = Capital Charges (capital invested X cost of capital).

Description: Economic Value Added can be complicated to calculate. The goal of EVA calculations is to determine the true economic profit of a company after taking into account the opportunity cost of capital invested. (More in a moment.)

Example: Your operating profit, after taxes, is $10,000. You have a $20,000 capital investment in the company; the opportunity cost of that investment (which means the money you could have earned if you invested the money elsewhere) is 10%.

Your capital charge is $20,000 X 10%, or $2,000.

$10,000 - $2,000 = $8,000. Your EVA, or economic profit, is $8,000.

EVA is admittedly a somewhat esoteric financial measurement. The goal of EVA is to take into account the fact that there is a "cost" to any capital invested in the company. If you have $50,000 and you invest that money in your company, you should receive a return, but you might not, at least not right away. But if you had invested the money in a Certificate of Deposit yielding 5%, you could make $2,500 per year in interest. So, in EVA terms, $2,500 is the cost of capital, and should be deducted from your operating profits to show your true profit.

Here's the bottom line. The goal of EVA calculations is to determine whether the company will generate a greater return on a capital investment than it could have received by investing the money elsewhere.

Say you have $8,000 you'd like to invest in website upgrades. You feel that investment will let you make $1,000 more profit each year. That sounds good, since you'll pay off the investment in five years, but let's factor in EVA.

You could invest the money in a Certificate of Deposit yielding 5%. There's no risk – you know you'll get that return. There is risk investing the money in your company – who knows what will happen. So, you decide you want to make at least 10% on your investment to mitigate some of the risk.

You give it some thought and decide to make the investment. And you make the $1,000 in additional profit you expected. But wait; your cost of capital is $8,000 X 10%, or $800. $1,000 - $800 is $200; that's your true economic profit. While you did make money, you didn't make as much as you hoped; in theory it will now take forty years to pay back the investment, once you factor in opportunity cost.

The goal of EVA is to answer this question: Does the investment truly add value to the company and generate profits that outweigh the risk?

Reference Link:
http://www.investopedia.com/terms/e/eva.asp

76. Accounts Payable Turnover Ratio (APT)

Equation: APT = TSP/AAP

Where TSP = Total Supplier Purchases, and

AAP = Average Accounts Payable.

Description: Accounts Payable Turnover indicates the frequency of payment of accounts payable (money owed suppliers and other vendors). The lower the ratio, the slower the company is paying off suppliers; a higher ratio indicates the company is paying off suppliers more quickly.

Example: You purchase commodities from wholesalers that you sell on your website. Each year you average making $150,000 in purchases. At any given time your average accounts payable (invoices you have received from those suppliers that you have yet to pay) equals $40,000.

150,000 / 40,000 = 3.75. Your APT is 3.75.

First let's talk about accounts payable. Any money you owe can be considered an accounts payable, but in this instance we're limiting your accounts payable to the money you owe on purchases from suppliers. (You could use APT to measure any type of accounts payable; if you wanted, you could evaluate your total electric expense against your average electric bills sitting in accounts payable.) Make sure you compare apples to apples, and measure a certain type of spending against accounts payable amounts related to that spending.

In the example above, your APT was 3.75. Say you tend to pay invoices on an average of twenty days from receipt. If you increase your payment time to thirty days, your average accounts payable will increase and your APT will decrease. That could mean you're hanging on to your cash longer so it can work harder for you, or it could mean you're struggling to pay your bills in a timely fashion.

All other considerations being equal, the higher your APT ratio, the more wisely you're using your money (unless your suppliers start to get upset.) But a high APT ratio could be an indication of cash flow problems. Use APT as a starting point for evaluating the health of your operations, and then dig a little deeper.

Reference Link:
http://www.investopedia.com/terms/a/accountspayableturnoverratio.asp

77. Accounts Receivable Turnover (ART)

Equation: ART = NCS/AAR

Where NCS = Net Credit Sales, and

AAR = Average Accounts Receivable.

Description: Accounts Receivable Turnover indicates the frequency of payment on accounts receivable (money owed to you by your customers you are waiting to "receive"). Since, in effect, a credit sale is like a loan, the lower the ratio, the slower your customers are paying off their "loans." The higher the ratio, the more quickly you're being paid.

Example: Last year your net sales, based on credit, were $100,000. (You don't take payment by credit card; you send invoices.) The average of your receivables at any given time was $25,000.

100,000 / 25,000 = 4. Your ART was 4.

Keep in mind a credit card sale is not "credit" for the purposes of this metric; while the customer is using credit, you are paid right away. The credit card company is the one extending credit, and that credit is a receivable for *them*, not you. So, if you sell products online and take credit card payments, your receivables should be almost nonexistent; you get paid before you ship any product.

But if your website yields customers who purchase goods or services through the use of credit (like if you are given a purchase order or if you send an invoice), the money you are owed is considered a receivable. If you're a consultant and you perform a service and bill the client later, the bill is a receivable – it is money you are owed but have not been paid.

Most businesses define payment terms, which is how long the customer has to pay the invoice. You may ask for payment on receipt, or within fifteen days, or thirty days – whatever makes sense for your business, offset by what your customers are willing to agree to. (If your terms are too tight, some customers may find another vendor who is willing to offer more generous terms.)

A typical standard is the expectation of payment within thirty days of the invoice date, although many companies focus on reducing the terms to fifteen days or less. Even if you specify "net 15" terms, meaning you expect payment within fifteen days of receipt of invoice, the entire process may take longer, you may take days to generate the invoice, then process the payment and deposit it, all of which increases your average accounts receivable.

Your goal is to increase your ART as much as possible; that way you have more cash flow and more cash on hand to fund operations. (Besides, why wait for your money.) Most businesses try to decrease APT and increase ART; that makes them "slow to pay and quick to receive." You can also increase your ART by requiring initial deposits; if a customer pays 50% of the invoice up front, the receivable for that customer is instantly cut in half.

Investors also pay attention to ART; if ART is five days or less, investors will typically be impressed by the efficiency of your billing and accounts receivable operations.

Reference Link: http://kpilibrary.com/?s=accounting

78. Quick Ratio (QR)

Equation: QR= QA/CL

Where QA = Quick Assets, and

CL = Current Liabilities.

Description: The Quick Ratio is sometimes called the liquidity ratio or the acid test ratio. It measures the liquidity of a company by determining the ratio between current liabilities and assets that can be converted into cash quickly. (Hence the term "quick ratio.") Inventory is excluded from liquid assets, since one of the goals of the QR is to determine if current liabilities can be paid without selling inventory.

Example: You have $10,000 in cash and $5,000 in liabilities.

10,000 / 5,000 = 2.0. Your QR is 2.0, meaning you have twice as much liquid assets as you need to pay off current liabilities. (That's a good thing.)

The QR is just what it sounds like – a quick way to measure the short-term health of a company and its assets.

A company with a QR lower than 1.0 may not be able to meet debt obligations without taking drastic measures like selling assets or borrowing additional funds. (Which creates another problem, because lenders are often unwilling to make loans to a company with a QR below 1.0; if the company is struggling to meet current liabilities, adding more debt may only aggravate the problem.)

The QR is in no way an absolute measure of business health; it does indicate whether a company can come up with funds in hours or days without selling inventory or hard assets. A company with a high QR is relatively solvent and has some buffer against short-term cash flow problems.

Reference Link:
http://www.valuebasedmanagement.net/methods_quick_r atio.html

79. Proprietary Ratio (PR)

Equation: PR = TSE/TTA X 100

Where TSE = Total Shareholder Equity, and

TTA = Total Tangible Assets.

Description: Shareholder funds include equity share capital, like shares of stock. Total assets include all business assets. The Proprietary Ratio indicates the percentage of company assets that were contributed by shareholders.

Example: The company has total assets of $10,000. Shareholder equity is $4,000.

4,000/10,000 = .4, or 40%. The company's PR is 40%.

The PR provides a sense of the overall financial strength of a company, and how sound the capital structure is. The higher the PR, the more solvent the company tends to be, because assets were purchased by using shareholder funds instead of through borrowing.

On the other hand, if the PR is too high that could indicate that cheaper sources of financing may not have been explored. Since borrowing can often be cheaper over the long term than selling stock, net profits may be lower due to the higher cost of acquiring capital.

So, like most things in life, a relatively high PR is good; too high is bad. In general terms, PR should be higher than 33%, which means shareholder funds add up to more than 33% of total assets. That will help the company be less dependent on outside sources of financing; if the ratio is lower, that could indicate that long-term loans may be somewhat at risk.

Reference Link:
http://basiccollegeaccounting.com/financial-ratio-proprietary-ratio/

80. Break Even Point (BEP)

Equation: BEP = FC/CPU

Where FC = Fixed Cost, and

CPU = Contribution Per Unit.

Description: In simple terms, a Break Even Point is when gains equal losses. (Spending $5,000 and making $5,000 means you broke even.) Where an investment is concerned, the BEP occurs when the investment yields a positive return.

Example: You invest $5,000 in new shipping equipment. The equipment allows you to package and ship golf clubs for $1 less per shipment than previously. Excluding considerations like interest payments on the $5,000, you'll need to ship 5,000 golf clubs to break even on your investment.

5,000/1 = 5,000. Your BEP is 5,000.

BEP can be used to evaluate a wide variety of situations. Say you decide to give an employee who writes blog posts a $1 raise, from $15 to $16 per hour. You hope the higher pay will serve as motivation and increase his productivity. If before the raise he was able to create and post 10 blog articles per hour, the cost per post was $1.50. If his productivity does not increase after his raise, his new cost per post is $1.60; effectively your cost per blog post has increased by almost 7%. If you hope he will reduce your cost per post to $1.40, he'll need to post 11.4 articles per hour for you to break even on his higher pay rate.

If that seems complicated, here's an easier example. You write and sell e-books. If it costs you $4,000 to produce the e-book (including being paid for your time, for text layout, etc.), and you sell the e-book for a profit of $10 per e-book (after deducting for expenses like web hosting, pay-per-click advertising, etc.), you need to sell 400 e-books to break even on your investment. (4,000/10 = 400.) Can you sell more than 400? Then you'll make money. If you don't think the market supports that level of sales, you won't make money.

Break-even analysis is a quick way to evaluate whether a project or investment makes sense. It can also tell you how *long* it will take to break even on an investment: If you install a $1,000 air conditioner that cuts your electric bills by $100 a month, it will take ten months to break even on the purchase; after that, the savings go into your pocket.

Reference Link:
http://www.12manage.com/methods_break-even_point.html

81. Actual Overhead Rate (AOR)

Equation: AOR = (OC/DC) X 100

Where OC = Overhead Costs, and

     DC = Direct Costs

Description: Actual Overhead Rates are often used by manufacturers and retailers to apportion overhead costs to projects or to products and services. Knowing your overhead rates lets you manage your operations better and benchmark your performance against other firms in your industry.

Example: Each month you spend $10,000 on direct costs like supplies, salaries, shipping costs, etc. You also spend $4,000 on overhead: Items like rent, heating and air conditioning, and office supplies.

4,000/10,000 = .4. Your Actual Overhead Rate is .4; for every dollar you spend on direct costs, you spend .40 on overhead costs.

Overhead is often seen as a necessary evil. While it would be nice to only spend money on direct costs like inventory, shipping, and salaries, every business has some amount of overhead costs – even if it's just the cost of hosting your website. The lower your overhead, the better your profits tend to be. (That's right – put the new stapler back on the office supply store's shelf.)

The key is to determine whether your overhead costs are rising or falling over time. While you could simply measure your overhead in raw dollars spent, that approach could be misleading. For example, say last month you spent $400 on overhead costs. This month you spent $500. The trend is in the wrong direction, right? Maybe not. Possibly this month your volume doubled and you worked more hours, so as a result you had $5,000 in direct costs instead of the $3,000 you spent last month. Last month your AOR was .13; this month it is .1. Your AOR declined, mainly because your overhead costs were spread across higher direct cost spending. Your AOR trend is actually moving in the right direction.

Tracking AOR over time also helps you account for unusual fluctuations in spending or activity. By the end of the year you'll have a good sense of your average AOR – and what steps you can take to lower your overhead costs.

Reference Link:

http://www.inc.com/welcome.html?aw=600&ah=600&destination=http://www.inc.com/articles/2000/05/18841.html

82. Gross Profit Margin (GPM)

Equation: GPM = (R – COGS) / R X 100

Where R = Revenue, and

COGS = Costs Of Goods Sold.

Description: GPM determines the percentage of gross profits your company has made. If your GPM is 40%, that means you make .40 for every dollar in sales.

Example: You sell bean bag chairs. Your gross sales last year were $100,000. The bean bags cost you, including shipping, $40,000.

$100,000 – 40,000 = $60,000; 60,000 / 100,000 = .60, or 60%. Your GPM is 60%.

If you produce a product, GPM can also help you understand how efficiently you use labor and raw materials; the lower your COGS, the higher your gross profit margin. Or, if you find a cheaper supplier for a product, your GPM will increase. And, if you raise prices, your GPM will increase. (Wouldn't it be nice to lower costs and raise prices at the same time?)

Companies with high GPMs tend to be more liquid since less of their money is tied up in production and inventory. If your GPM is declining, it's probably due to risings costs and competitors who are putting pressure on your prices.

GPM calculations can be used in a number of ways; at least three methods are very useful. One method is to simply track your GPM over time; it will help you sense check your operations and your competitive position in the marketplace. Another use of GPM is to measure yourself against other companies in your industry; after all, if you sell software, the average GPM is typically in the 80% to 90% range; if you sell grocery items, your GPM is likely to be a single-digit percentage.

Finally, you can calculate the GPM for individual products. Say you sell two products: Product A has a GPM of 70%, and Product B has a GPM of 40%. Product B is less profitable; if higher volume doesn't make up for lower GPMs, it could make sense to focus your marketing efforts on Product A... or to find ways to reduce your COGS on Product B so the GPM falls more into line with Product A.

Reference Link:
http://ri.medialsaude.com.br/static/enu/parametros_contabeis.asp

83. Net Profit Margin (NPM)

Equation: NPM =NP/TS X 100

Where NP = Net Profit, and

TS = Total Sales.

Description: The Net Profit Margin indicates the level of profit per dollar of revenue. Net profits are profits on sales after expenses, overhead, and payments on liabilities. Think of NPM this way: It measures not just what you earn but what you *keep* (until you pay taxes, of course).

Example: You had total sales of $20,000 this month. You made a net profit (after expenses) of $2,300.

2,300 /20,000 = .115, or 11.5%. Your Net Profit Margin is 11.5%.

NPM is a good way useful to compare companies in similar industries, or to compare your current results against past results. A higher NPM indicates you're doing a good job of lowering costs and increasing operating efficiency.

NPM also helps you compare apples to apples. Say last year you had total sales of $40,000; you made $10,000 in net profit. Your NPM was 25%. This year your sales doubled to $80,000, and your net profit increased to $18,000. Great – but your NPM fell to 22.5%. While that may be due to increased costs that you can't control (or don't want to control), it could be due to the fact your operations are less efficient. While you did manage to increase your net income – which is a good thing – your profit margins fell.

Again, that might be a good result: If total sales and total profits increased because you lowered your prices, your NPM will naturally decrease – but you may be happy to make that tradeoff if your profits rise dramatically.

If your NPM falls make sure it's as a result of good business decisions you've intentionally made.

Reference   **Link:**

http://www.accountancy.com.pk/refratio.asp?type=1

84. Interest Coverage Ratio (ICR)

Equation: ICR= EBIT/IE

Where EBIT = Earnings Before Income Taxes, and

IE = Interest Expense.

Description: The Interest Coverage Ratio measures how well a company can meet interest payments on outstanding liabilities.

Example: Your company has interest payments totaling $50,000. Your earnings for the same period (before taxes) are $130,000.

130,000/50 = 2.6. Your Interest Coverage Ratio is 2.6; that means you can meet your interest payments 2.6 times.

A high ICR could indicate a company is not taking advantage of opportunities to increase earnings by leveraging debt. On the other hand, an ICR below 1.0 means the company is not generating sufficient earnings to meet interest payments.

Since failing to meet interest payments tends to result in default, ICR is a critical measure used by lenders. Keep in mind ICR can measure short-term conditions; if you evaluate your ICR on one month's earnings and interest, you may over- or under-state a company's long-term ICR.

Some industries average higher ICRs than others. If your business is cyclical – for example, if you sell products that are in high demand during the Christmas season – your ICR can vary widely throughout the year. Make sure you evaluate your ICR over time to factor in normal swings in business. You'll know you're on the right track if your ICR gradually increases, unless you decide to take on more debt in order to expand, offer new products, or purchase new equipment or software to increase operating efficiencies.

Reference Link: http://cpaclass.com/fsa/ratio-01a.htm

85. Profitability Index (PI)

Equation: PI= PV / IV

Where PV = Present Value of future cash flow, and

IV = Initial Value of investment.

Description: The Profitability Index is a way to evaluate a project's potential return. (Typically PI is used to evaluate capital projects.) The goal is to evaluate future cash flows against the cost of the initial investment.

Example: You decide to purchase new servers to store customer data. The investment totals $20,000. You project the present value of future cash flow to be $25,000.

25,000/20,000 = 1.25. The investment will yield a PI of 1.25.

Would you decide to invest in a project with a ratio below 1.0? Hopefully not; that means the return is less than the investment. As the PI goes up, the attractiveness of the project increases, too. In short: The higher the PI the better.

Let's compare two projects. Project A requires a cash investment of $15,000. You estimate the present value of future cash flows to be $16,000. Divide 16,000 by 15,000; the PI is 1.066.

Project B requires a cash investment of $9,000, and the present value of future cash flow is $9,900. Divide 9,900 by 9,000; the PI is 1.1.

PI measures the ratio between cash flow and investment. All other considerations being equal, Project B is the better project, at least in terms of return.

Reference Link:
http://en.wikipedia.org/wiki/Profitability_index

Bibliography

Accountancy. "Profitability Ratios." Accountancy.com. <http://www.accountancy.com.pk/refratio.asp?typ e=1>

Accounting Parameters." Medial Saude. <http://ri.medialsaude.com.br/static/enu/parametro s_contabeis.asp>

"Accounting Ratios for Financial Statement Analysis." CPAClass.com. <http://cpaclass.com/fsa/ratio-01a.htm>

Alexa.com. Free Traffic Metrics, Top Site Lists, Site Demographics, Hot URLs, and More. The Web Information Company. <www.Alexa.com>

"Calculation of the Point at Which the Gains Equal the Losses. Explanation of Break-even Point Analysis." 12Manage. <http://www.12manage.com/methods_break-even_point.html>

Chef, Tad. "33 Website Success Metrics Instead of Rankings, Google PageRank and Traffic." SEOptimize. August, 2008. <http://www.seoptimise.com/blog/2008/08/33-website-success-metrics-instead-of-rankings-google-pagerank-and-traffic.html>

Chow, Theresa. "eCPM – What Exactly is That?" Blogspot.com. February, 2006.

<http://adsense.blogspot.com/2006/02/ecpm-what-exactly-is-that.html>

"Cost Per Action (CPA)." MarketingTerms.com. <http://www.marketingterms.com/dictionary/cost_per_action/>

Custer, Ken. "Marketing Metrics: Where to Get Them? Which Ones Work?" Ad-Mkt-review.com. <http://www.ad-mkt-review.com/public_html/docs/fs059.html>

Demand Metric. <http://www.demandmetric.com/content/practical-tools/website-design-budget>

Edit-X. "Search Engine Visibility: Do You Measure Up?" <http://www.search-visibility.com/>

Eisenberg, Brian. "20 Tips to Minimize Shopping Cart Abandonment, Part 1." Clickz.com. August, 2003. <http://www.clickz.com/2245891>

"Establish Metrics." Edgar Web Design Guide. <http://eserver.org/courses/w01/tc510/edgar/Denise/denise9.htm>

"Financial Ratios." NetMBA. <http://www.netmba.com/finance/financial/ratios/>

"Financial Ratio: Proprietary Ratio." <http://basiccollegeaccounting.com/financial-ratio-proprietary-ratio/>

Gamse, Philippa. "Metrics Matter!" StreetDirectory.com. <http://www.streetdirectory.com/travel_guide/100 20/web_development/metrics_matter.html>

Gold, Kevin. "Know These Three Performance Metrics to Increase Website Sales." ConversionChronicles.com. <http://www.conversionchronicles.com/Know_Th ese_Three_Performance_Metrics_to_Increase_We bsite_Sales.html>

Goldenberg, Gabriel. "Repeat Visitors: Tracking > Percentage vs Absolute Numbers." SEORoi.com. July, 2008. <http://seoroi.com/case-studies/repeat-visitors-tracking-percentage-vs-absolute-numbers/>

Google Answer. "What's the Difference Between Clicks, Visits, Visitors, Pageviews, and Unique Views?" Google. <http://www.google.com/support/analytics/bin/ans wer.py?hl=en&answer=57164>

"How Do I Calculate My Overhead Rate?" Inc.com. May, 2000. <http://www.inc.com/welcome.html?aw=600&ah =600&destination=http://www.inc.com/articles/20 00/05/18841.html>

Investopedia. ---"Accounts Payable Turnover Ratio." Investopedia.com.

<http://www.investopedia.com/terms/a/accountspayab
leturnoverratio.asp>

---"Debt Service Coverage Ratio – DSCR."
Investopedia.com.
<http://www.investopedia.com/terms/d/dscr.asp>

---"Economic Value Added – EVA."
Investopedia.com.
<http://www.investopedia.com/terms/e/eva.asp>

---"Return On Investment (ROI)."
<http://www.investopedia.com/terms/r/returnonin
vestment.asp>

IT Toolbox. "Build Your Knowledge Sharing Network."
<www.ittoolbox.com>

"IBM Informix Backup and Restore Guide." IBM.
<http://publib.boulder.ibm.com/infocenter/idshelp/
v10/index.jsp?topic=/com.ibm.bar.doc/barmst46.h
tm>

Jasra, Manoj. "Measuring Visitor Engagement and
Behavior." SearchEngineGuide.com. October,
2006. <http://www.searchengineguide.com/manoj-
jasra/measuring-visit.php>

---"Are You Measuring Visitor Engagement and
Behavior?" SearchEngineguide.com. July, 2006.
<http://www.searchengineguide.com/manoj-
jasra/are-you-measuri.php>

Kennon, Joshua. "Return on Assets (ROA): Investing Lesson 4 – Analyzing an Income Statement." About.com. <http://beginnersinvest.about.com/cs/investingless ons/l/blreturnonasset.htm>

KPI Library. "Accounting." <http://kpilibrary.com/?s=accounting>

---"Backup." <http://kpilibrary.com/categories/backup>

---"Key Performance Indicators." <http://kpilibrary.com/categories/systems>

---"Marketing." <http://kpilibrary.com/?s=marketing>

Lake, Laura. "Marketing During a Recession." About.com. <http://marketing.about.com/>

Manion, Josh. "Tracking Onsite Search." Stratigent. <http://www.stratigent.com/web-sight-newsletter/web-analytics-newsletter-archive/tracking-onsite-search/default.html>

Marketing Budget Planner 2006: Benchmarks and Key Performance Indicators." MarketResearch.com. <http://www.marketresearch.com/product/display.asp?productid=1263406&xs=r&g=1&curr=USD&kw=&view=toc>

"Mean Time to Provision." KnowledgeTransfer.net. <http://www.knowledgetransfer.net/dictionary/ITIL/en/Mean_Time_to_Provision.htm>

Novo, Jim. "Turning Customer Data into Profits with a Spreadsheet." <http://www.jimnovo.com/metrics-definitions.htm>

---"Web Site Traffic Metrics." <http://www.jimnovo.com/metrics-definitions.htm>

---"Visitor Quality: Audience/Content Match." <http://www.jimnovo.com/metrics-definitions.htm>

Numion. "Stopwatch." <http://www.numion.com/Stopwatch/index.html>

"Quick Ratio Model – A Method for Measuring Liquidity." <http://www.valuebasedmanagement.net/methods_quick_ratio.html>

"Performance Metrics." Ezineads.com. <http://www.ezineads.info/frequently-asked-questions>

Peterson, Eric T. "How to Measure Visitor Engagement, redux." WebAnalyticDemystified.com. October, 2007. <http://blog.webanalyticsdemystified.com/weblog/

2007/10/how-to-measure-visitor-engagement-redux.html>

PublicInsight.com. "Getting Down to the Right Numbers, Part 3: Churn, Churn, Churn! Does Your Website Have Too Much Bounce?" <http://www.publicinsite.com/Reports/churn-churn-part3.asp>

Rowland, Emory. "RealMetrics Web Hosting Metrics." Blog.Clickfire.com. <http://blog.clickfire.com/realmetrics-web-hosting-metrics/>

Russer, Michael. "Boost Site Profitability by Measuring Visitor Behavior." RealtyTimes.com. February, 2008. <http://realtytimes.com/rtpages/20080207_boostsite.htm>

SpectrumInc.com. "Visitor Behavior." <http://www.spectruminc.com/website-analytics/visitor-behavior.aspx>

---"Brand Development." <http://www.spectruminc.com/internet-marketing-strategy/brand-development.aspx>

SpeedyAdverts. "Web Site Loading Time." <http://www.speedyadverts.com/SATopics/html/web_site15.html>

Symantec. "Encrypting Critical Backup Data."
January, 2007.
<http://www.symantec.com/business/resources/art
icles/article.jsp?aid=encrypting_critical_backup_d
ata>

WebPublicitee.com. "Site Statistics, Web Site Traffic
Statistics, Visitor Analysis, Unique Visitor,
Tracking Visitor and Unique Web Visitor
Statistics."
<http://www.webpublicitee.com/Visitor-
tracking/index.html>

Webmaster World. "Top Rank Online Marketing."
<http://www.webmasterworld.com/webmaster/349
6869.htm>

WebsiteCEO. "Average Order Size."
<http://www.websiteceo.com/screenshots/hitlens/0
9.htm>

Website Optimization.com. "Average Web Page Size
Triples Since 2003."
<http://www.websiteoptimization.com/speed/twea
k/average-web-page/>

---"Higher Traffic and Speed Guaranteed."
<http://www.websiteoptimization.com/services/an
alyze/ >

Wen, Bo. "Supporting Minimum Bandwidth Guarantee
for Shared LightPath Traffic in VPN Over WDM
Networks."

<http://www.eecs.wsu.edu/~dawn/Slides/MBG
-OWns.ppt>

Wikipedia. "A/B Testing."
   <http://en.wikipedia.org/wiki/A/B_testing>

---"Benefit-cost Ratio."
   <http://en.wikipedia.org/wiki/Benefit-cost_ratio>

---"Click-through Rate."
   <http://en.wikipedia.org/wiki/Click-through_rate>

---"Customer Lifetime Value."
   <http://en.wikipedia.org/wiki/Customer_lifetime_
value>

---"Mean Time to Repair."
   <http://en.wikipedia.org/wiki/Mean_time_to_repai
r>

---"Page Rank."
   <http://en.wikipedia.org/wiki/PageRank>

---"Profitability Index."
   <http://en.wikipedia.org/wiki/Profitability_index>

---"Return on Marketing Investment."
   <http://en.wikipedia.org/wiki/Return_on_marketin
g_investment>

www.ingramcontent.com/pod-product-compliance
Lightning Source LLC
Chambersburg PA
CBHW051529170526
45165CB00002B/666

* 9 7 8 1 4 4 9 5 2 2 1 4 8 *